NATURE AND CULTURE
IN WESTERN DISCOURSES

NATURE AND CULTURE IN WESTERN DISCOURSES

STEPHEN HORIGAN

ROUTLEDGE
London and New York

First published in 1988 by
Routledge
11 New Fetter Lane, London EC4P 4EE

British Library Cataloguing in Publication Data

Horigan, Stephen, 1953-
   Nature and culture in Western Discourses.
   1. Social anthropology. Theories
   I. Title
   306' .01
   ISBN 0-415-00798-4

Typeset by LaserScript Limited, Mitcham, Surrey.
Printed in Great Britain

To F.E.N.

Contents

Acknowledgements

This text began as a doctoral thesis and has culminated in a book. The process has been a lengthy one, and I have benefited greatly from the comments and suggestions of a great number of people. I would particularly like to acknowledge the following: Nadine Cartner and Dave Morley, for their friendship and continual support over many years; Ted Benton, Ian Craib, and Maxine Molyneux of the University of Essex, who all read drafts of the manuscript, as did John Gagnon of the University of New York, Stoneybrook. I am especially indebted to Mark Cousins and Paul Hirst, not only for reading the entire manuscript, but also for their encouragement and patience, and their willingness to discuss countless times the arguments that follow. While all of the above have played a part in shaping the ideas in this book they are not, needless to say, responsible for its errors.

Introduction

> Then, Hermogenes, I should say that this giving of names can be be no such light matter as you fancy, or the work of light or chance persons; and Cratylus is right in saying that things have names by nature, and that not every man is an artificer of names, but he only who looks to the name which each thing by nature has, and is able to express this name in letters and syllables.[1]

The opposition between nature and culture has a long history in western thought. Among other sources it can be found in classical philosophy. Plato's dialogue the *Cratylus* is concerned with the relationship between words and things: Cratylus advances the thesis that language accurately reflects the world because words represent the essential nature of things. That is, there is a natural relationship between words and what those words represent. In contrast, Hermogenes argues that names are merely the result of convention and agreement: there is no necessary relationship between words and the objects named in language. The dialogue starts with Socrates questioning Hermogenes' claims for the absolute conventionality of language. The latter had expressed his views thus:

> I... cannot convince myself that there is any principle of correctness in names other than convention and agreement; any name which you give, in my opinion, is the right one, and if you change that and give another, the new name is as correct as the old... for there is no name given to anything by nature; all is convention and habit of the users.[2]

But if language is purely conventional, Socrates argues, if the meaning of words is solely the product of the immediate and individual context in which they are used – i.e., if a man could be called a man by one speaker and a horse by another – then it would be impossible to distinguish truth from falsity or wisdom from folly. The fact that wise men and fools exist demonstrates that both wisdom and folly have their own essence, an essence which is captured by language. This process of describing reality, the act of naming, is the work of the dialectician, one skilled in the use of words.

1

Socrates, then, secures agreement for the views of Cratylus, that names must, by definition, accurately reflect the essence of the objects named in language. Moreover, the sounds themselves, if they are to name an object, must resemble that object. It is here that Socrates challenges Cratylus. Through a discussion of the qualities of the sounds of different Greek dialects it is established that the name given to an object might vary according to the dialect, i.e. that sounds having different qualities might represent the same object. Cratylus agrees that the explanation for this lies in custom, which as Socrates points out is none other than convention:

> If this is true, then you have made a convention with yourself, and the correctness of a name turns out to be convention, since letters which are unlike are indicative equally with those which are like, if they are sanctioned by custom and convention. . . . I quite agree with you that words should as far as possible resemble things; but I fear that this dragging in of resemblance, as Hermogenes says, is a kind of hunger, which has to be supplemented by the mechanical aid of convention.[3]

Having rejected Hermogenes' view of the absolute arbitrariness of language Socrates establishes at least his partial vindication by acknowledging the role of convention in determining meaning. But the dialogue ends inconclusively, and the opposition between nature and convention remains unresolved. Nature versus convention, *physis* versus *nomos*; the opposition between nature and culture has become an integral part of western metaphysics.

In the seventeenth and eighteenth centuries the distinction between nature and culture took on a wider significance. Political philosophers used a transition from a state of nature to one of culture to account for the institution of political society, the mechanism of transition being a social contract. In *Leviathan* Thomas Hobbes described the state of nature, 'the natural condition of mankind', thus:

> In such condition, there is no place for Industry; because the fruit thereof is uncertain: and consequently no Culture of the Earth; no Navigation, nor use of the commodities that may be imported by sea. . . no account of Time; no Arts; no Letters; no Society; and which is worst of all, continuall feare, and

2

danger of violent death; and the life of man, solitary, poore, nasty, brutish, and short.[4]

The desire to secure the greater liberty of all ensured that individuals would give up their 'right to all things', or rather would transfer that right to a sovereign authority, a 'visible Power to keep them in awe, and tye them by feare of punishment to the performance of their Covenants'.[5]

Similarly, John Locke used a state of nature and a social contract as analytical devices for specifying the basic rules of political obligation:

> The great and chief end therefore, of men's uniting into
> commonwealths, and putting themselves under government,
> is the preservation of their property: to which in the state of
> nature there are many things wanting.[6]

For Rousseau the passage from nature to culture functions as a means for understanding the true nature of humanity; and in Condillac's *An Essay on the Origin of Human Knowledge* the oppositions between nature and culture and human and animal were used to demarcate the field of the social, marking out a specific field of study for the human sciences. The concept of the state of nature was not intended to represent an actual historical state, but a conjectural one, a philosophical device used for specifying the attributes of humanity. Rousseau makes this clear at the beginning of the *Discourse on the Origins of Inequality Among Men*;

> I have here entered upon certain arguments, and risked some
> conjectures, less in the hope of solving the difficulty, than
> with a view to throwing some light upon it, and reducing the
> question to its proper form. . . . For it is by no means a light
> undertaking to distinguish properly between what is original
> and what is artificial in the actual nature of man, or to form
> a true idea of a state that no longer exists, perhaps never
> existed, probably never will exist; and of which it is,
> nevertheless, necessary to have some true ideas in order to
> form a proper judgement of our present state.[7]

These conceptions, of culture as opposed to nature and the human as distinct from the animal, have been handed down from the

Enlightenment to the contemporary human sciences, and remain a central part of modern social theories.

But what is the function of these oppositions in the human sciences?[8] My argument is that the opposition between nature and culture has been used as one attempt to 'ground' the human sciences, to legitimize and justify their existence as autonomous disciplines. On the one hand the distinction provides the human sciences with their own object and justification - culture. On the other hand it provides a principle of demarcation, of what is not culture and of what, therefore, does not fall within the human sciences. This has been done by marking out culture as a self-enclosed and unified realm of phenomena set apart from, and opposed to, natural/biological phenomena: a separate 'level' of reality. Culture becomes definitive of the human species: that is to say, the possession of culture sets humans apart from animals. As Leslie White has written,

> The cultural category, or order, of phenomena is made up of events that are dependent upon a faculty peculiar to the human species, namely, the ability to use symbols. These events are the ideas, beliefs, languages. . . customs. . . and institutions that make up the civilisation – or culture. . . of any people.[9]

Culture, then, becomes the object of the human sciences. As a consequence the human sciences have sought to stress and defend the autonomy of culture as a uniquely human realm resting essentially on the ability of humans to impose meaning on the world through the use of symbols. Culture defines the human and language becomes the sign, *par excellence*, of culture.

It is this idea of culture which I want to examine and question in this book. I start by looking at the role played by the opposition between nature and culture in cultural and social anthropology respectively. The work of three American cultural anthropologists, A.L. Kroeber, Leslie White, and Marshall Sahlins may be taken as exemplary in this respect. Their work can be seen in the context of a number of important trends in late nineteenth-century social thought which provide the context for the development of the modern anthropological concept of culture. Within this the work of Franz Boas must be considered. One of his primary concerns, as it was later of Kroeber, was to effect the separation of the categories of race and culture. In doing this, by carving out culture as a distinct area of study (by arguing that cultural phenomena could only be understood in terms of culture) they both undercut the theoretical premise of eugenics and racial anthropology, that is, that the cultural and historical achievements of a people were a product of their racial composition; they thereby helped to establish anthropology as a theoretically independent institution in the human sciences.

This idea that culture is an attribute unique to 'man' is inextricably linked to a second idea: that culture is to be seen as a realm of signification dependent upon the ability to use and construct symbols. Both of these ideas find expression in the work of Leslie White and Marshall Sahlins. For White, as the quotation above has shown, culture becomes elevated, reified to a privileged position, an autonomous causal order of society, itself the subject of a specific form of enquiry, culturology: the 'science of culture'. For Sahlins, the encircling of culture as a realm of meaning, the exclusive preserve of 'man', functions as a means for the defence of a symbolic anthropology in its rejection of the unwanted attentions of functionalist and utilitarian attempts to explain the social world.

My choice of these writers for consideration is deliberate. They are of course major figures in American anthropology: Kroeber, as one of the first of Boas's students, was central in establishing anthropology as a credible discipline, and he was one of the prime movers in developing a theory of cultural determinism in the 1920s, which was to dominate American anthropology for nearly fifty years. Leslie White rose to prominence in the 1940s and 1950s, at a time when anthropology was undergoing considerable expansion in America, and he became an important influence on the emerging generation of young anthropologists. Marshall Sahlins has, in a number of books written in the last twenty years, established himself as one of the foremost anthropologists. All three writers can be seen as a product, to a greater or lesser extent, of the Boasian approach to anthropology: Kroeber was one of Boas's students; White studied under two of Boas's former students, Alexander Goldenwieser and Edward Sapir; and Sahlins was a student of White's.

But this idea of culture is not restricted to American cultural anthropology. Despite the obvious differences in approach the same sorts of issue arise in the work of Claude Levi-Strauss. In *The Savage Mind* Levi-Strauss is concerned with systems of thought and forms of 'primitive' classification. The categories of nature and culture, he argues, are a product of the necessity of the human mind to conceptualize reality in terms of binary oppositions. As such, they are universal, existing across cultures; they are fundamental aspects of human thought. In the *Elementary Structures of Kinship* the opposition between nature and culture is seen as instrumental in explaining the function of the incest taboo. Levi-Strauss argues that the taboos on incest that all societies observe make social life - culture - possible by prohibiting possible natural sexual relationships and introducing the rule of exogamy. Thus culture, rule-governed behaviour, is a direct consequence of the operation of the incest taboo on marriage practices. Perhaps the case is somewhat different with Levi-Strauss because what is at stake is not so much the absolute distinction between nature and culture, as the fact that for him culture always involves a distinction between nature and culture. Nevertheless some at least of the same problems occur.

On an empirical level, all the anthropologists discussed require the maintenance of an opposition between nature and culture, which in turn rests upon the existence of essential differences between humans and animals. The distinction between nature and culture is then always bound up at a certain point with the distinction between human and animal. But the problems involved in the use of such oppositions as that between nature and culture are not simply empirical, not merely questions as to where exactly the boundary should be drawn (whether between humans and animals or between primates and non-primates), they are also conceptual. The distinction between nature and culture is invoked as the means by which the phenomenon of culture is constituted as a field of study. But the distinction itself is not the product of enquiry; it is, rather, the condition of enquiry. As a consequence the distinction functions as the means whereby a certain metaphysical argument is smuggled in. So the object of investigation of the human sciences is still itself caught up in a certain metaphysics.

This metaphysics of the distinction can be traced historically. If one considers the history of themes of primitivism and wildness, and of stories of feral children, it is clear that while conceptions of the human and of the animal have always been important in western culture - 'savages' are discussed by Homer, and the first recorded example of a wild man in western literature is that of Enkidu, in the Babylonian epic of Gilgamesh[10] - the question of marking out the terms of these distinctions with any degree of certainty has always been problematic. The important point about the figures of the savage and the wild man is that they straddle the very boundary between nature and culture, the human and the animal. There is always a discomforting confusion between the two. The very existence of the savage obscures the distinctions; at times he is confused with the mythological creatures of the ancient world, the satyrs, centaurs, dog-headed men, etc. The wild man, while being of human culture, is set apart from it, inhabiting the world of nature, a nature moreover seen in terms of both danger and freedom. Specifying the terms of the oppositions between nature and culture, human and animal only becomes an exercise of scientific importance during the eighteenth century, with the birth of the human sciences and the appearance of 'man' as an object of study. Here the qualities and attributes specific to 'man' become the object of empirical dispute, and the 'policing' of the boundary between nature and culture becomes a decisive issue for the human sciences. This is why so much philosophical attention is focused on stories of feral children, on the relationship between humans and the newly discovered anthropoid apes, and on the native inhabitants of 'savage' societies. As with the savage and the wild man the feral child constitutes a problem for the distinction between nature and culture; such children are seen as providing the means by which the essential qualities of mankind are demarcated from those of animals. With the re-emergence of the issue of the biological limits of human behaviour versus its social determination in the twentieth century, such cases again become important. The great reluctance of social scientists like Levi-Strauss, and others, to admit of the possible existence of feral children (he dismisses them as 'cultural monstrosities', 'congenital defectives') stems from a desire to maintain a qualitative distinction between nature and culture, human and animal; to maintain claims for the autonomy of culture and the uniqueness of human behaviour.

Perhaps the most vivid contemporary version of these issues lies in the passionate debates concerning language use amongst chimpanzees. I am not concerned to decide between the various sides in the dispute; indeed, I think that the central issue in these debates – to what extent have chimpanzees learned a human language – is a profoundly misplaced one. Rather, my intention is to show how the oppositions between nature and culture, human and animal are implicated in the framing of the various positions taken. What is remarkable is the persistence of these oppositions; oppositions which are perhaps more of an obstacle than the foundation of knowledge in the human sciences.

Works quoted in the text are referenced in the Notes near the end of the book. A bibliography which appears after this gives much fuller reference to the sources used.

1
Nature and culture in American cultural anthropology

Nineteenth century anthropology, it is often claimed, can best be characterized by its commitment to unilinear evolutionism: the belief that all societies move through a set of determinate developmental stages and that this movement, or evolution, is in a single direction; the measure, of course, is always to the standards reached by European civilization. A problem with this characterization is that the notion of unilinear evolution belongs more properly to eighteenth century rather than nineteenth century social thought. The belief, born of the Enlightenment, that all peoples could progress through the same cultural and evolutionary stages to the pinnacles of civilization was by no means universally accepted in the nineteenth century. While the commitment to social evolutionism was present there were many who believed that some of the more 'savage' varieties of humankind would never ascend to the pinnacle of the evolutionary scale, lacking as they did the necessary 'fitness' to survive. George Stocking quotes one contemporary writer, Franklin Giddings, who claimed that there was 'no evidence that the now extinct Tasmanians had the ability to rise. They were exterminated so easily that they evidently had neither the power of resistance nor any adaptability.'[1]

Lacking the commitment to progressive optimism that characterized its eighteenth century counterpart, Victorian anthropology was less concerned with the future development of a universal human nature than in tracing the historical forms that had led some human groups to the higher stages of civilization exemplified by western European societies. In the course of this development some groups displayed more adaptability and thus made more progress, while others reached the limits of their possibilities and either remained in that condition or succumbed to environmental conditions and died out completely.[2]

For the purposes of the present argument then, the main difficulty with Victorian anthropology was not that its evolutionism was (or was not) unilinear, but that, as Peter Reynolds, in *The Evolution of Human Behaviour* has argued, it was not properly evolutionary, in the sense in which we understand the term today. Evolution, he writes,

> is pre-eminently a historical concept that recognises the great possibilities for change in both the products of nature and the works of man, and it sees these changes as part of a historically continuous chain of events. It is a dynamic conception of nature and history most explicitly developed in the nineteenth century by Darwin and by Marx. The evolutionism of Victorian anthropology, in contrast, was a typological framework which did not emphasise the process of historical change but the ranking of enduring forms on a scale of temporal progression.[3]

Thus, although contemporaneous with Darwin, Victorian anthropology operated with a different conception of evolution, one related to an older tradition associated with the 'comparative' history of the eighteenth century: all known existing societies represent various stages in the overall development of humanity. By using the comparative method an understanding of the general historical development of humanity could be reached, even if gaps in the chain existed - that is to say, if some of the historical stages were not actually present. Given this approach, Reynolds argues, 'the application of the comparative method in anthropology became the specification of the characteristics of each historical stage.'[4]

Thus there is no necessary connection between evolutionary biology, as developed by Darwin, and the evolutionism of Victorian anthropology; they are logically distinct. It must be admitted, however, that Darwin himself was ambiguous on the issue of human evolution. While the core theory of *The Origin of Species* was one of evolutionary transformation, without any implications of 'higher' or 'lower' forms, Darwin's attempts to deal with this question in *The Descent of Man* (1871) clearly shows the influence of the anthropological evolutionism of his contemporaries. Unable to provide reliable fossil evidence for his theory of human evolution from anthropoid ancestors, Darwin fell back on the belief, derived from the eighteenth century, and still very much a part of contemporary understanding, of a hierarchy of human races.

> At some future period, not very distant as measured by centuries, the civilized races of man will almost certainly exterminate, and replace, the savage races throughout the world. At the same time the anthropomorphous apes . . . will no doubt be exterminated. The break will then be rendered wider, for it will intervene between man in some more civilized state . . . than the Caucasian, and some ape as low as a baboon, instead of as at present between the negro or Australian and the gorilla.[5]

Thus the publication of Darwin's work had a contradictory effect on late nineteenth century social theory, particularly upon anthropological questions concerning the problem of race. On the one hand, the arguments in *The Origin of Species* served to undermine the theoretical basis for the racism inherent in polygenist thought which claimed that the various non-white races were the product of a separate creation and were not related to Europeans - an argument often used to justify slavery. On the other, despite noting forcefully in a notebook written in 1837 that 'It is absurd to talk of one animal being higher than another'[6] his arguments in the *Descent of Man* concerning the emergence of *Homo sapiens* from apes (leaning as they did towards evolutionist assumptions), gave a scientific credibility to a number of racist implications. As Greta Jones notes, Darwin

> resurrected a graduated chain of development from ape to man and it was possible to combine this with theories of inherent difference and inferiority . . . Darwin's *Descent of Man* was an attempt to find a graduated series of links - mental, social and moral - as evidence for evolution. To this exigency, a belief in human equality, to which other areas of Darwin's life and work testify, was sacrificed.[7]

Racist anthropology then, could find in the *Descent* support for the view that non-white or non-western peoples were a throw-back to a more primitive and brutish stage of human development, a good deal further back on the road to civilization. Anthropologists like A.C. Haddon used arguments like this to justify Britain's imperialistic expansionism:

11

the statement that the most efficient peoples must ultimately prevail may be accepted as correct. The racial, economic, social and political history of South Africa affords us a striking example of this process in the mutual relations of Bushman, Hottentot, Bantu, Boer and Briton.[8]

The popularity and success of Darwin's evolutionary theories also served to strengthen the influence of biology on social theory. This is not to suggest that this influence did not already exist. On the contrary, as Greta Jones has demonstrated, the complex of theories known as Social Darwinism were the product of already existing assumptions in Victorian social thought. Nevertheless, the publication of Darwin's work lent a degree of credibility to them and provided inspiration for a number of theorists dedicated to championing the cause of biology in the determination of social life.

Foremost among these was Sir Francis Galton, the founder of the eugenics movement, a movement that became, in the words of Richard Hofstadter, 'the most enduring aspect of Social Darwinism'.[9] Galton was the half cousin of Darwin whose influence on the development of his thought he readily declared. Indeed, he explicitly stated that the aim of eugenics was to 'see what the theory of heredity, of variations and the principle of natural selection mean when applied to man'.[10]

The eugenics movement was founded on a belief in the inheritance of moral and intellectual characteristics, as well as on physical ones and in the law of natural selection operating accordingly. Galton and his followers argued for the application of the practice of the selective breeding of domesticated animals to human groups so that those properties in a population deemed most desirable or favoured should be singled out and encouraged to multiply faster than, and at the expense of, less desirable ones, thus improving the 'racial stock' of the population.

Galton's belief in the operation of natural selection on intellectual and moral qualities was accompanied by his doctrine of the differing capabilities of racial groups. As Derek Freeman has noted 'Galton was convinced that all of the differences between "savage" and "civilized" societies could be explained by the "innate character of different races".'[11] And he quotes Galton's statement: 'Every long-established race has necessarily its peculiar fitness for the conditions under which it has lived, owing to the sure operation of Darwin's law of natural selection.'[12]

Of course these ideas were not new; the 'racial interpretation of history' - the view that the mentality and level of intellectual development of a people was dependent upon its racial characteristics - has been traced back to the Count de Gobineau, whose book *Essai sur l'inégalité des races humaines* was published in 1853. Indeed, Gobineau's book was itself a reworking of the biological classification of races developed in the eighteenth century by Linnaeus. What was new about Galton's work was that with the advent of the eugenics movement he was able to incorporate these beliefs into a programme of social reform. In England in 1905 the University of London set up a chair in eugenics, and in 1907 Galton established the Eugenics Education Society to further his cause. In a lecture given in the same year Galton predicted the possibility of proclaiming, in the not too distant future, 'a "Jehad" or Holy War against customs and prejudices that impair the physical and moral qualities of our race.'[13]

In the United States too, Galton's ideas were becoming increasingly influential, probably more so than in Britain. A National Conference on Race Betterment held in 1914 demonstrated the growing influence of eugenic ideas in the major social and medical institutions of American society. In 1907 Indiana became the first American state to introduce a sterilization law, and by 1915 twelve states had adopted similar laws. As Derek Freeman has noted, by the beginning of the First World War nearly fifty American universities including Harvard, Cornell, and the Massachusetts Institute of Technology offered lectures or courses about eugenics.[14]

This brief discussion of the popularity of Galton's work is instructive, for it was the institutionalization of eugenic ideas that so disturbed Franz Boas, and became the main target of his criticism around the turn of the century.

When Boas entered anthropology in the early 1880s it was dominated by an approach known as evolutionary naturalism, best exemplified by the work of E.B. Tylor. Evolutionary naturalism was based on two main principles: first, that all human cultures developed in a uniform way according to the same evolutionary principles; second, that culture was determined by the same laws of nature as material life, was therefore part of a natural process, and was therefore amenable to scientific analysis. Tylor, in *Primitive Culture*, wrote,

> the history of mankind is part and parcel of the history of nature . . . our thoughts, wills and actions accord with laws as definite as those which govern the motion of waves, the combination of acids and bases, and the growth of plants and animals.[15]

It is a commonplace in histories of the discipline to identify Tylor as the founder of modern anthropology, and to trace back to him the origins of the modern concept of culture. Indeed, Tylor's definition,

> Culture or civilisation, taken in its wide ethnographic sense, is that complex whole which includes knowledge, belief, art, morals, law, custom, and any other capabilities and habits acquired by man as a member of society.[16]

is the most widely quoted in textbooks on the subject. Stocking, however, argues persuasively that Tylor merely transferred to anthropology, or to his particular form of social evolutionism, the traditional humanist or literary notion of culture evident in the work of writers such as Matthew Arnold. By making 'culture' synonymous with 'civilization', Tylor's ethnocentrism demonstrates the lack of cultural relativism that is crucial for modern anthropology, for he is referring to the degree rather than the type of civilization evident in a society: as Stocking says:

> 'Civilisation', for Tylor as for Lewis Henry Morgan, was the highest stage in an explicitly formulated sequence of progressive human development which began in 'savagery' and moved through 'barbarism'. Inherited from the late eighteenth century, this sequence - and the 'hierarchy of values' it implied - was central to Tylor's ethnology.[17]

Tylor's thought was infused with the eighteenth century notion of progress, the belief that all human cultures would inevitably achieve, through progressive evolution, the levels reached by European civilization, which though not itself perfect, was, in Tylor's words, 'at least what is most perfect in human achievement.'[18] Savagery and barbarism were merely lower stages or levels of the civilization reached by European nations.

According to Tylor,

> Civilisation actually existing among mankind in different
> grades, we are enabled to estimate and compare it by positive
> examples. The educated world of Europe and America
> practically settles a standard by simply placing its own
> nations at one end of the social series and savage tribes at the
> other, arranging the rest of mankind between these limits
> according as they correspond more closely to savage or to
> cultured life .... Thus on the definited basis of compared
> facts, ethnographers are able to set up at least a rough scale of
> civilisation. Few would dispute that the following races are
> arranged rightly in order of culture: Australian, Tahitian,
> Aztec, Chinese, Italian.[19]

The modern anthropological concept of culture, however, is
relativistic and pluralistic: there is no 'hierarchy of values' and
there are no 'higher' or 'lower' forms of civilization: all peoples are
equally 'cultured'. The jump from Tylor's definition of culture,
with its evolutionist assumptions and its implied relations of
inferiority and superiority, to the concept understood by modern
anthropology, so forcefully argued for by Kroeber, Lowie, and
others, first began to take shape in the writings of Franz Boas.
Stocking writes,

> In extended researches into American social science between
> 1890 and 1905, I found no instances of the plural form in
> writers other than Boas prior to 1895. Men referred to
> 'cultural stages' or 'forms of culture', as indeed Tylor had
> before, but they did not speak of 'cultures'. The plural
> appears with regularity only in the first generation of Boas'
> students around 1910.[20]

It is perhaps strange, at first sight, that Boas should have been so
opposed to the evolutionary naturalism of men like Tylor, with its
declaration that anthropology be seen as a branch of biology - the
science of life - and that the phenomena of human culture should be
studied according to the principles and methods of the natural
sciences, for Boas was himself trained as a physicist. His doctoral
thesis, written while at the University of Kiel, was on the colour of
sea water. But he soon became disillusioned with what he termed
the 'materialistic Weltanschauung', and left physics to pursue an

interest in ethnology. Having studied philosophy under Benno Erdmann, and read - and by all accounts heard[21] - Wilhelm Dilthey, both leading neo-Kantians, Boas was unsympathetic to the evolutionary naturalism that pervaded anthropology at the time, with its crude application of Darwin's theory of natural selection to cultural phenomena. He preferred instead Dilthey's view that the cultural or human sciences could not be subsumed under the natural sciences as they rested upon different foundations. Rejecting the progressive developmentalism of evolutionist anthropology, Boas argued that specific cultures were the result of specific historical processes, of the diffusion and borrowing of elements from other cultures. No culture developed in complete isolation, the cultural achievements of a society depended upon the particular historical and social experiences of that society; there was no one uniform model of cultural evolution.

The realization of such diversity convinced Boas that it was unlikely that cultural phenomena could be explained by the simple application of the laws of natural selection, and led him to a belief in the necessity of studying culture in its own terms. In 1900, in his presidential address to the American Folklore Society, he argued that, being independent of natural forces, cultural phenomena should be studied independently of biology. Such a view, however, inevitably brought him into conflict with the hereditarian ideas of the eugenicists. The increasing popularity of Galton's eugenics in the United States brought with it a hardening of attitudes and a radicalization of the claims being made for the movement. From 1883, when Galton initially advanced the 'vastly preponderating effects of nature over nurture',[22] the claims of the eugenicists increased steadily, until in 1915 Paul Popenoe, the editor of the *Journal of Heredity*, asserted that 'heredity is not only much stronger than any single factor of the environment, in producing important human differences, but is stronger than any possible number of them put together.'[23]

In addition to the growing success of eugenics was the resurgence of interest in 'scientific' racism, sparked off by the publication, in 1915, of Madison Grant's *The Passing of the Great Race*, and an English translation of the Count de Gobineau's *The Inequality of Human Races*, a year later. The main principle of 'scientific' racism, it will be remembered, was that the cultural or intellectual achievements of a people are determined by its racial composition. It was in opposition to theories such as this, which conflated the categories of race and culture, that Boas had published *The Mind of Primitive Man* in 1911. His objective was to distinguish culture from race, thus establishing the independence of the former. It was varying social and historical conditions, he said, and not the biological character of a race, that determined its culture:

> The biological constitution does not make the culture. It influences the reactions of the individual to the culture. As little as geographical environment or economic conditions create a culture, just as little does the biological character of a race create a culture of a definite type . . . . Culture is rather the result of innumerable interacting factors and there is no evidence that the differences between human races . . . have any directive influence upon the course of development of culture.[24]

Thus Boas's insistence upon defending the independence of cultural phenomena brought him into direct confrontation with the increasingly biologically determinist ideas of the hereditarians, and heightened the tension between the opposing theoretical positions that was to lead to the nature/nurture controversies and to the emergence of cultural determinism. As Stocking has remarked of Boas,

> The whole thrust of his thought was in fact to distinguish the concepts of race and culture, to separate biological and cultural heredity, to focus attention on cultural process, to free the concept of culture from its heritage of evolutionary and racial assumptions, so that it could subsequently become the cornerstone of social scientific disciplines completely independent of biological determinism.[25]

This point of Stocking's is important, for as well as opposing the views of racial anthropologists and eugenicists, Boas was determined to defend the independence of anthropology as a specifically social science. Indeed, he was instrumental in institutionalizing anthropology as an academic discipline in the United States and was concerned to protect its autonomy from what he clearly regarded as the biological imperialism of his critics. Hence the need to distinguish the concepts of race and culture and to seek an explanation of cultural phenomena in their own terms. As Cravens has noted,

Boas and his students realized that they must create a body of autonomous theory for their science; their rebellion against the domination of ethnological or social science theory by the concepts, the metaphors, and assumptions of the natural sciences, then, was a logical consequence of their efforts to transform anthropology into a respected science and profession in America.[26]

Thus, in an attempt both to counter the racist theories of eugenicists and racial anthropologists, and to advance the claims of anthropology as an independent discipline, Boas argued forcefully for the separation of the categories of race and culture. One consequence of this separation however, and one not completely apparent in his work (appearing first in that of his students, such as Kroeber and Lowie), was the development of the modern anthropological concept of culture. In this, culture is seen as a self-enclosed and unified realm of phenomena, a distinct level, or order, of society rigidly differentiated from biological or psychological phenomena. The development of the concept of culture led, inevitably, to the emergence of cultural determinism, an approach to theory which stresses the social or cultural determination of human behaviour to the complete exclusion from consideration of biological or psychological factors. Freeman points out that Kroeber and Lowie devised

a doctrine quite as extreme as that of their hereditarian opponents. It was expressed in the formula *omnis cultura ex cultura*, which, in asserting that cultural phenomena can be understood only in terms of other cultural phenomena, was predicated on the existence of an unbridgeable chasm between biology and cultural anthropology, and so inexorably involved an absolute cultural determinism.[27]

While Kroeber and Lowie were principally responsible for the development of cultural determinism, its emergence was made possible by the work of Franz Boas. Through his critique of evolutionary anthropology and eugenics, Boas laid the groundwork for the development of modern anthropology

Thus it was that when other social scientists looked to the 'science of anthropology' for guidance on the issues upon which it might be presumed to speak authoritatively, it was the Boasian viewpoint to which they turned . . . . Sociologists, many of whom had themselves been developing explanations of human behaviour along analogous lines, found these explanations legitimised by the anthropological idea of culture, which increasingly was incorporated into the vernacular of their own discipline.[28]

It is against this background, then, that the development of American cultural anthropology must be seen; and within this development the work of A.L. Kroeber, Leslie White, and Marshall Sahlins. In the remainder of this chapter I want to show how, in these three writers, the conception of culture that was beginning to take shape in the work of Franz Boas developed into an organizing principle of the contemporary human sciences, serving to define the parameters of anthropological theory.

A.L. Kroeber: 'The Superorganic'

Though born in New Jersey, in 1876, Kroeber, like Boas, was of German descent; the influence of the German Enlightenment, particularly the philosophical heritage of Kant and Goethe, was strong in his family. Like Boas also, Kroeber came to anthropology late, having begun his academic career lecturing in English before receiving the first Ph.D. in anthropology from Columbia. His essay 'The Superorganic', first published in the *American Anthropologist* in 1917, stands as a landmark in the history of cultural anthropology. The essay, which represented, in Kroeber's words, a 'declaration of independence', a manifesto for the emergent movement of cultural determinism, hinges on establishing the argument for the rigid separation of nature and culture, and thereby the existence of culture as an autonomous realm - the 'superorganic'. In so doing, the essay, like the Boasian project in general, performs the dual function of both undercutting the theoretical basis for the racism of eugenics - by distinguishing 'race' from 'culture' - and, by proclaiming culture as an independent level of reality, championing the cause of anthropology as an academic discipline.

In a later introduction to the essay written in 1952 Kroeber states that he was less concerned with combating forms of biological determinism of sociocultural phenomena on the part of biologists than clearing up the confusions caused by 'the blind and bland shuttling back and forth between an equivocal "race" and an equivocal "civilisation"', and of challenging a set of philosophical assumptions 'that left precarious the autonomous recognition of society, and still more that of culture.'[29] This refusal to acknowledge the independence of the social was the result, Kroeber argues, of a confusion between the realms of nature and culture - in his words the 'organic' and 'social' - a confusion brought about largely by the popularity of Darwinian theory, and the attempts to explain the evolution of human cultures with recourse to the concepts of evolutionary biology. Here Kroeber displays his distrust of evolutionary theory, a distrust he shared with Boas; in 1910 it was Kroeber's belief that human beings were 'apparently exempt from the operation of the laws of biological evolution.'[30] Darwinian concepts cannot be used to explain the evolution of culture, he argues, because the realm of the social is the product of a different type of evolution; there are two separate forms of evolution; of the organic and of the social, and these operate according to two different principles; the principle of transformation with respect to organic phenomena, and that of accumulation, in the field of the social:

> A bird is born with a pair of wings, but we have invented the aeroplane. The bird renounced a potential pair of hands to get his wings: we, because our new faculty is not part of our congenital make-up, keep all the organs and capacities of our forefathers but add to them the new ability. The process of the development of civilisation is clearly one of accumulation . . . . In organic evolution, the introduction of new features is generally possible only through the loss or modification of existing organs or faculties.[31]

In animal species growth occurs through changes in the organic constitution of the organism, whereas the growth of human cultures occurs through invention, diffusion, etc., without any organic changes. Kroeber's argument here, on the existence of two radically different types of evolution depends upon his claims as to the existence of essential and fundamental differences between human and animal. So the distinction between nature and culture or organic and social is overlaid upon another distinction, that between human and animal. This latter distinction does not inhere in the greater intelligence of humans - indeed intelligence is itself a product of the distinguishing feature - but the fact that humans possess culture, 'the indispensible condition of what is peculiarly human.'[32] 'In civilisation man has something no other animal has.'[33] Here Kroeber is using the terms 'culture' and 'civilization' synonymously, as is clear from his comments in the 1952 introduction referred to earlier: 'That my "superorganic" of 1917 referred essentially to culture is clear not only from all the concrete evidence cited but from the constant use of "civilisation", "culture", "history", and their adjectival forms.'[34]

That the possession of culture by humans represents an absolute difference is also made clear by the following: 'The distinction between animal and man which counts is not that of the physical and mental, which is one of relative degree, but that of the organic and social which is one of kind.'[35]

Kroeber finds justification for these claims in the fact that humans possess language, for it is language that signals the existence of culture, the mark of humanity: 'the difference between the so-called language of brutes and that of man is infinitely great.'[36]

Although an attribute specific to humanity, culture is not part of an individual's make-up, but is external to the individual. A French child brought up in China by Chinese parents would speak not French, but Chinese. Kroeber is here making the argument for the separation of race and culture: while racial characteristics - colour of hair, eye shape, etc. - remained the same, cultural factors, that is language, would be affected: 'No amount of association with Chinese would turn our young Frenchman's eyes from blue to black, or slant them, or flatten his nose .... His eyes and his nose and his hair are his from heredity; his language is non-hereditary.'[37]

The fact that language is non-organic demonstrates that, in terms of human culture, a separate principle operates: to all intents and purposes then, humanity is the product of a separate creation. Kroeber uses the example of isolated children to demonstrate his argument:

> place on a desert island ... two or three hundred human infants ... leave them in total isolation from their kind; and what shall we have? The civilisation from which they were torn? .... No, not any fraction; nor a fraction of the civilisational attainments of the rudest savage tribe. Only a pair or a troop of mutes, without arts, knowledge, fire, without order or religion.[38]

21

Kroeber's formulation here is somewhat reminiscent of Durkheim: culture is external to the individual, literally 'superorganic':

> ... tradition, what is 'given through', handed along, from one to another, is only a message. It must of course be carried; but the messenger after all is extrinsic to the news . . . tradition is something super-added to the organisms that bear it, imposed upon them, external to them.[39]

The fact that the possession of culture sets humans apart from animals indicates something about Kroeber's view of humanity:

> The essential difference between animal and man, in this illustration, is not that the latter has finer grain or the chaster quality of material; it is that his structure and nature and texture are such that he is inscribable, and that the animal is not.[40]

The view with which we are presented here is the *tabula rasa* of Lockean empiricism: humanity is 'a tablet that is written upon.'[41]

It was the confusion between the organic and the social, argued Kroeber, that led to the popularity of both the Lamarckian doctrine of the inheritance of acquired characteristics, and eugenics. The former, which in another essay he had called 'theoretically, biological heresy',[42] had enjoyed a return to favour among biologists even though, according to Kroeber, August Weissmann had disproved it in the 1880s. The attraction of the Lamarckian doctrine was that it avoided the unacknowledged differences between biological and social evolution, and the fact that the latter depended not upon the inheritance of acquired characters, but on socially transmitted knowledge. According to Stocking, Kroeber was 'virtually alone among social scientists in realising what had been the implications of Lamarckianism for the independent development of the social sciences.'[43]

And Derek Freeman has remarked that Kroeber was aware that 'the rejection of Lamarckian doctrine was an essential precondition for the scientific study of culture.'[44]

As we have already seen, the eugenics movement, like Lamarckianism, gained in popularity in the first two decades of the twentieth century. Its programme, racial 'improvement' through selective breeding, was, according to Kroeber, 'a fallacy'. The question to be asked, he argued, was to what extent social phenomena could be collapsed into the organic: 'If the social is something more than the organic, eugenics is an error of unclear thought.'[45] The mistake of men like Galton and Pearson was in 'the failure to distinguish between the social and the mental.'[46] According to Kroeber, 'Mentality relates to the individual. The social, or cultural, on the other hand, is in its essence non-individual. Civilisation, as such, begins only where the individual ends.'[47]

The theories of Darwin and Mendel operate with respect to a population of individuals, but for Kroeber, 'a thousand individuals do not make a society.'[48] The essence of the social is that civilization, rather than being merely an 'aggregate of psychic activities' is also an 'entity beyond them'.[49] The whole is more than the sum of its parts. Not only that, but the nature of the social is such that its appearance is 'without antecedents in the beginnings of organic evolution.'[50] The social is a product of a separate evolution. 'The dawn of the social thus is not a link in a chain, nor a step in a path, but a leap to another plane.'[51]

As noted above, Kroeber's arguments for maintaining the distinction between nature and culture, and for the separation of the categories of race and culture, not only served an institutional function - to protect the interests of anthropology as an academic discipline - but also an important political one, by providing an urgent criticism of the racism of much social and anthropological thought. But however positive and important the intentions, the manner in which they were realized has led to a number of serious consequences for the further development of anthropology. For the maintenance of a rigid opposition between nature and culture resulted in a notion of culture premised upon an essentialist conception of the human. Kroeber's arguments produced a transcendent notion of culture - culture as a reality *sui generis*.

Kroeber's argument depends upon his claim that language and culture are unique to humans, and that language, although specifically human, is not part of an individual's biological make-up, but is 'external' to the individual. In earlier essays Kroeber had argued that there existed 'nothing homologous to the rudest culture or civilisation'[52] in any animal species. Culture is 'both superindividual and superorganic', is 'that which the human species has and other social species lack.'[53] However, from what we now know about non-human primates it is clear that culture, in the sense of shared and learned patterns of behaviour, has been shown to exist - in a rudimentary form perhaps, but exist nonetheless - in a number of other species. Research on Japanese macaque monkeys, the observations of wild chimpanzees by Jane Goodall, and the ape-language experiments (the subject of a later chapter) all demonstrate that the making of claims for human uniqueness, the attempts to draw a circle around the human and maintain arguments that begin 'only humans can ...' is a precarious exercise.

Kroeber's second claim, as to the nature of human language, is not without its problems either. The American linguist Noam Chomsky has argued strongly that language cannot be understood purely in cultural terms. While Chomsky would be sympathetic to Kroeber's claim that language is specific to humans - indeed, in *Rules and Representations* he states his belief to that effect - he rejects a culturalist type of explanation, and asserts that the ability to use language is wired into the neural mechanisms of the human brain. Now, although Chomsky maintains a belief in the uniqueness of human language, it is not necessary to do so in order to argue for the importance of biological factors. The theory put forward by the psychologist Eric Lenneberg (examined in greater detail in a later chapter), of the existence of a critical period for the acquisition of language, linking it with the maturation of the brain, originated as an attempt to explain the development of the call systems of songbirds. The important point is that modern research in both psychology and linguistics seriously undermines the extreme environmentalism of Kroeber.

Kroeber's work appeared nearly seventy years ago, before any serious research on non-human primates; but the fact that his arguments have remained so important in anthropology demonstrates that what is at stake is less a factual dispute than an ideological disagreement. As we shall see, the effect of such dogmatism continues to exert a stranglehold on social theory.

Leslie White: 'The Symbol'

Like A.L. Kroeber before him, Leslie White was a product of the school of anthropology pioneered by Franz Boas. White studied at the New York School for Social Research, and at Chicago, under two of Boas' former pupils, Alexander Goldenweiser and Edward Sapir. Although White later became strongly critical of Boas, especially of his anti-evolutionism, in his own insistence on seeing culture as a self-enclosed and autonomous realm, and his commitment to a radical cultural determinism, he remained very much within the Boasian tradition. Like Boas and Kroeber also, he became one of the most respected and influential anthropologists of his generation. One commentator describes him as 'one of the major instruments by means of which anthropology became a fully-fledged science.'[54] White was at his peak intellectually in the period immediately following the Second World War, a period which saw a rapid growth in anthropology, and thus his influence on the generation of young anthropologists studying in the 1950s was considerable.

White's move away from and eventual rejection of Boas's anti-evolutionism was the result of a number of factors: his growing interest in the work of Morgan, who was much vilified by the Boasians at the time for his evolutionism and whom he read while teaching at the University of Buffalo; a trip to the Soviet Union in 1929 where he encountered the writings of Marx and Engels, and their use of Morgan; lastly, his experience of trying to justify anti-evolutionism in classes with students at Buffalo, who, belonging to a later generation did not share the general hostility towards evolution current in the anthropology of the time. White has claimed that his students increasingly refused to accept his arguments: 'Before long I realised that I could not defend the doctrines of anti-evolutionism; then I realised that I could no longer hold them; they were untenable.'[55]

From the early 1930s onwards then, White began to develop his ideas about cultural evolution. White's view of evolution as representing progress to a higher form - the nature of the process being one of increasing complexity - is, however, closer to Spencer than to Darwin. For White, as for Spencer, evolutionary changes are those that lead to greater differentiation of structure and specialization of function, whereas Darwin saw any change as evolutionary.

White applied these ideas to the evolution of human cultures, arguing for the possibility of locating cultures in an evolutionary scheme. His belief in the evolutionary development of culture led him to the conclusions, *contra* Boas and the cultural relativists, that not only could different cultures be compared objectively and ranked hierarchically, but that the evolution of culture, as a totality in itself, could be traced from 'its beginnings upon an anthropoid level to the present time.'[56] White, like Kroeber before him, defines culture as a distinct and autonomous level dependent upon the function of language, an attribute unique to the human species.

Culture constitutes an integrated system, an organized totality comprising of three sub-systems: technological, sociological, and ideological. The technological system consists of 'material, mechanical, physical and chemical instruments ... by means of which man ... is articulated with his natural habitat.'[57] This involves tools and machinery, means of subsistence, materials of shelter, etc. The sociological system is made up of social relations, patterns of behaviour: kinship, economic, military, political systems, etc; and the ideological system, of ideas, beliefs, knowledge, myths, legends, philosophies, etc.

These three sub-systems together combine to form a structured cultural order in a topography not dissimilar to the Marxist notion of the social formation as a complex social totality structured by the determination of the economic base. In the case of White's cultural system the role of determination is played by technology ('the material, mechanical means of adjustment to the natural environment'),[58] with social and ideological/philosophical factors as secondary and subsidiary systems:

> There is a type of philosophy proper to every type of technology .... A pastoral, agricultural, metallurgical, industrial, or military technology will each find its corresponding expression in philosophy. One type of technology will find expression in the philosophy of totemism, another in astrology or quantum mechanics.[59]

The primacy given to the role of technology is central here, for it is technology that provides, in White's words, 'A key to an understanding of the growth and development of culture',[60] and a means by which different cultures can be ranked objectively on an evolutionary scale. Cultures develop and evolve into structurally more complex forms as a result of the increasing efficiency and sophistication of their technological systems. One of the functions of culture is to provide for the continuation of the human species, by satisfying basic survival needs: of subsistence, protection, and social regulation etc. It does this through the control, regulation and development of energy. The amount of energy produced by a given culture 'will be proportional to the efficiency of the technological means with which the energy is put to work.'[61] This enables White to formulate what he calls 'the basic law of cultural evolution'; 'culture evolves as the amount of energy harnessed per capita per year is increased, or as the efficiency of the instrumental means of putting the energy to work is increased.'[62]

In what is perhaps his most famous essay, 'The Symbol', White attempts to clarify the concept of culture. Like Kroeber before him, White's aim is to defend the autonomy of culture, and he does this by maintaining the opposition between nature and culture and by making culture the attribute that marks off humanity from the rest of the animal world.

White's argument hinges on the importance of the symbol for it is the symbol that lies at the heart of his notion of the human:

> All human behaviour originates in the use of symbols . . . . It is the symbol which transforms an infant of *Homo Sapiens* into a human being; deaf mutes who grow up without the use of symbols are not human beings. All human behaviour consists of, or is dependent upon, the use of symbols. Human behaviour is symbolic behaviour; symbolic behaviour is human behaviour. The symbol is the universe of humanity.[63]

Furthermore, the ability to use and construct symbols is restricted to humanity; it marks off mankind from the rest of the animal world:

> The thesis that we shall advance and defend here is that there is a fundamental difference between the mind of man and the mind of non-man. This difference is one of kind, not one of degree . . . . Man uses symbols; no other creature does. An organism has the ability to symbol or it does not; there are no intermediate stages.[64]

The possession of this ability to use symbols locates essential differences between human and animal; the symbol is used as the key to culture:

> All culture (civilisation) depends upon the symbol. It was the exercise of the symbolic faculty that brought culture into existence and it is the use of symbols that makes the perpetuation of culture possible. Without the symbol there would be no culture, and man would be merely an animal, not a human being.[65]

So, White's argument, like Kroeber's, depends upon the existence of essential differences between human and animal: the possession of culture is specific to humanity because of its unique ability to use symbols. Culture is a distinct class of phenomena, a level of reality dependent upon symbols. It is an argument for human uniqueness, the difference between human and animal is a difference not of degree but of kind, a qualitative difference: animals lack the intelligence to use symbols. The ability, for example, that apes possess to use tools is not a symbolic tool use, as it is with humans - apes cannot pass on tool use from one generation to the next, they remain stuck in the present: the characteristic feature of their mental life is the 'extremely narrow limits' of the temporal world in which they live ... the ape lives in a small world ... temporally it is limited to the moment.'[66]

White's claim that the ape's use of tools is similarly confined to the here and now, is today a very difficult one to uphold, because of what we now know about the cognitive abilities of other primates (especially the chimpanzee researches of Jane Goodall). But White's position, like Kroeber before him, is not simply the product of an inadequate grasp of the facts of modern primate research, it is an ideological one, encumbered by the persistence of an outdated dogmatism. As late as 1975 White wrote that the claim that 'culture is a thing, or process, *sui generis* means just what it says: and (the claim that) "culture is to be explained in terms of culture" still holds.'[67]

Marshall Sahlins: *Culture and Practical Reason*

In *Culture and Practical Reason* Marshall Sahlins maintains the position that culture is an autonomous and uniquely human realm, a realm of signification dependent upon the ability to impose meaning on the world through the use of symbols. The book consists of a series of polemics against a variety of forms of what Sahlins terms 'practical reason'; that is to say, theories that seek the origins and explanations of culture by subordinating it to one or other dominant logic - material or adaptive advantage, functional necessity (of either a biological or an economic kind), utilitarian interest, etc. Sahlins groups these forms of practical reason into two broad categories:

i) *Naturalism*: the reduction of culture to the realm of instrumental necessity, providing for the maintenance of the human species through the satisfaction of biological needs. Here, the

disappearing act performed on culture consists of its absorption, one way or another, within nature. Either cultural practice is a behavioural mode of appearance of the laws of natural selection, just like any 'species-specific behaviour', or else it is subsumed within a more general ecosystem which alone and as a totality enjoys the powers of self-regulation or 'mind' and whose constraints are realised in cultural forms.[68]

ii) *Subjective utilitarianism*: whereby culture becomes the product of the rational calculations of a universalized 'economic man', the result of 'the purposeful activity of individuals in pursuit of their own interests and their own satisfactions.'[69] Thus a wide variety of social theorists including Morgan, the later Marx, and Malinowski, are criticised for locating the origins of the cultural order elsewhere, within the framework of another, superior, logic. As against these writers Sahlins cites the recognition of Boas and Levi-Strauss that the essence of culture lies in its symbolic qualities as a meaningful system. Thus rather than explain culture as a result of the maximization of means-ends relations, or of adaptive advantage (or biological necessity), Sahlins posits a 'cultural reason', the symbolic. The 'distinctive quality of man' is not 'that he must live in a material world, circumstances he shares with all organisms, but that he does so according to a meaningful scheme of his own devising, in which capacity mankind is unique.'[70]

Thus Morgan, for example, is described as a 'pre-symbolic anthropologist', for whom the intelligence of the human mind is 'simply rational rather than symbolic',[71] representing not a cultural logic actively constructing the social world, but a passive agency responding to and reflecting a practical/biological logic. Morgan's kinship classifications, Sahlins argues, are seen as simply the result of the recognition of the biological advantages of marriage practices, rather than as a product of a specifically social logic: thus, the superiority of Punaluan marriage (the exclusion of own sisters from the group of women shared by brothers and own brothers from the group of men shared by sisters) - 'for Morgan the triumph of biology in society'[72] - and then still later monogamy, as the 'highest' form of marriage, is an expression of the advantages of 'civilized' marriage practices over the original promiscuity of consanguineal unions of brothers and sisters with their resultant problems of inbreeding. This is the recognition of a naturally superior condition:

> The advantages were appreciated and the behaviours formulated as modes of organisation - for example, Punaluan family, the gens - which were in turn subject to secondary reflection or codification in kinship terminology. The general line of force in the argument, *the orientation of logical effect*, is from natural constraint to behavioural practice, and from behavioural practice to cultural institution:
> circumstance - practice - organization and codification (institution)
> To understand any given segment in the chain of effect, it is referred to the reason in the segment preceding: ... such that the total sequence represents the sedimentation within culture of the logic of nature (adaptive advantage).[73]

Sahlins calls Morgan a 'pre-symbolic anthropologist' because he ignores the unique human ability to use symbols - and therefore symbolic behaviour as the basis for human intellection - in favour of the continuity of intelligence between human and animal in which, for example, the mind of the human and the mind of the beaver are both rational, the difference being one of degree and not kind. Morgan's mistake, according to Sahlins, was to reduce language 'to the act of naming the differences manifest to experience. He preferred to respect the continuity of intelligence, at the expense of the creativity of language.'[74]

Similarly, argues Sahlins, for Malinowski culture is merely 'the instrumental realisation of biological necessities';[75] an artificial, and (Malinowski's words) 'secondary environment'; a means to an end, the end being to satisfy the biological needs of the human species. Thus culture, as the medium through which those needs are satisfied, becomes the product of functional necessity. Malinowski's functionalism is a classic example of making culture dance to the tune of practical interest by reducing a great diversity of bizarre and exotic customs to a functional practicality of either biological necessity or economic advantage. Material advantage is revealed as the underlying reason for the 'savage' practices of 'primitive' societies. So, the 'Intichiuma ceremonies of the Australian Aborigines', Malinowski claims, 'with their wild dances, their painted bodies and their symbolically carved shields actually performed a function in their economic life',[76] that is they improve economic organization. Rather than explain cultural phenomena in cultural terms Malinowski finds instead their explanation in terms of a practical, functional logic. But to reduce the content of cultural practices to the level of mere appearance, in favour of an underlying functional essence demonstrates a failure to grasp the complexities of such practices.

> Utilitarian functionalism is a functional blindness to the content and internal relations of the cultural object. The content is appreciated only for its instrumental effect, and its internal consistency is thus mystified as its external utility. Functionalist explanation is a kind of bargain made with the ethnographic reality in which content is exchanged for an 'understanding' of it .... There is an enormous disparity between the richness and complexity of cultural phenomena such as the Intichiuma and the anthropologist's simple notions of their economic virtues. Only the most infinitesimal fraction of that rich reality, and nothing of its specific content, is accounted for by its function.[77]

What Sahlins is objecting to here is the reductionism involved: the subordination of the symbolic logic of the cultural code to the practical logic of functional necessity. By denying the symbolic logic of cultural phenomena, Malinowski effectively reduces the role of culture to the handmaiden of utilitarian interest:

> Malinowski's elimination of symbol and system from cultural practices, this cannibalism of form by function, constitutes an epistemology for the elimination of culture itself as the proper anthropological object. Without distinctive properties in its own right, culture has no title to analysis as a thing-in-itself. Its study degenerates into one or another of two commonplace naturalisms: the economism of the rationalising individual (human nature); or the ecologism of selective advantage (external nature).[78]

Sahlins locates the failure of writers like Morgan and Malinowski in their inability to recognize the uniqueness of the human use of symbols and the place of the symbol as definitive of a cultural order defined as a meaningful system. This failure makes for the possibility of viewing culture not as in itself the main object of the anthropologists' concern, but rather as an instrument for the realization of biological or economic forces.

All these types of practical reason have also in common an impoverished conception of human symboling. For all of them, the cultural scheme is the *sign* of other 'realities', hence in the end obeisant in its own arrangement to other laws and logics. None of them has been able to exploit fully the anthropological discovery that the creation of meaning is the distinguishing and constituting quality of men.[79]

Forms of practical reason predominate not only in ethnographic descriptions of 'primitive' societies, however, Sahlin argues. Bourgeois economics, for example, provides an account of production in contemporary capitalist societies in the terms of classic utilitarianism: culture is seen as a result of practical interest, and the economy as a process of material maximization, as the product of individuals acting to further their own interests. The economy is an arena of pragmatic action where commodities are produced to satisfy material wants and needs. But although biological needs must be met, although production must provide for the biological continuation of the species, it does so according to a cultural scheme which is never the only one possible. Practical reason cannot explain the cultural order, but vice versa, 'functional value is always relative to the given cultural scheme.'[80]

Production, therefore, is something more and other than a practical logic of material effectiveness. It is a cultural intention. The material process of physical existence is organised as a meaningful process of social being.[81]

The cultural order is a unity, a symbolic structure whose unity is given by meaning; it is signification that defines function. The error of functional and utilitarian accounts of culture is to ignore the fact that it is the cultural code that determines the utility of a commodity and therefore what is produced. Food preferences and the clothing system, Sahlins argues, are two examples that demonstrate the cultural determinants of production. Production, he writes, 'is the realisation of a symbolic scheme.'[82] So a symbolic logic is at work which governs production, the production of clothing deemed appropriate for given individuals in particular situations - for men as opposed to women, adults as opposed to adolescents, clothes appropriate for work or for wearing 'around the house':

In manufacturing apparel of distinct cut, outline, or colour for women as opposed to men, we reproduce the distinction between femininity and masculinity as *known* to this society.

That is what is going on in the pragmatic-material process of production.[83]

Similarly, with respect to eating habits: there is nothing 'natural', or obvious about the fact that Americans refuse to eat dogs or horses, but readily consume cattle - or even, within the latter, value highly certain parts of the animal's flesh ('meat', 'steak') while considering other parts inferior (tongue, kidneys, etc.). It is the cultural code that defines edibility: 'It is this symbolic logic which organizes demand. The social value of steak or roast, as compared with tripe or tongue is what underlies the difference in economic value.'[84]

Sahlins is right to challenge the explanatory claims of functionalist and utilitarian accounts of culture; to reject the reductionism involved in conceiving of culture as the by-product of biological or economic necessity. But the cost of his argument is too high a price to pay. His adherence to a specifically *symbolic* definition of culture as an autonomous, meaningful system, the exclusive property of humanity, commits him to the sterile dualism that results from opposing nature to culture and that sets human apart from animal. This dualism does nothing to further his critique of reductionist theories of culture: on the contrary, it merely essentializes the categories of the human and of culture, and remains a stumbling block to the advancement of knowledge in the human sciences.

2
Nature and culture in the work of Levi-Strauss

It is perhaps not surprising that of all the human sciences it is anthropology that has been most concerned with the opposition between nature and culture; or that, within anthropology, that the opposition has most frequently been associated with the writings of Claude Levi-Strauss. For Levi-Strauss has, in a sense, made the opposition his own. And while he has at times sought to distance himself from it, to undermine it, he has been unable completely to dispense with it, and the opposition remains a central thread in his work. Jacques Derrida has pointed to this ambivalence in Levi-Strauss' writings towards the opposition, suggesting that it is an inevitable consequence of employing a set of concepts derived from a system of metaphysics that one is attempting to criticize.

> *There is no sense* in doing without the concepts of metaphysics in order to attack metaphysics. We have no language - no syntax and no lexicon - which is alien to this history; we cannot utter a single destructive proposition which has not already slipped into the form, the logic, and the implicit postulations of precisely what it seeks to contest.[1]

In this chapter we shall see that Levi-Strauss is indeed still caught up in this metaphysical circle; that his use of the opposition between nature and culture displays some of the same problems that were encountered in the work of the American cultural anthropologists. The discussion will centre upon two texts, *The Savage Mind*, in which the opposition functions as a central element within a general system of classification; and *The Elementary Structures of Kinship*, where it provides the mechanism for the origins of society.

The Savage Mind registers a pause in Levi-Strauss' thought between his earlier work on kinship structures and his later interest in myths and symbolism. Published in 1962, the book represents the second stage of an examination started in a previous text, *Totemism*, into the nature of human thought. Explaining the concept of 'totemism' - the use of and identification with natural species or inanimate objects as a means for representing the similarities and differences between social groups - had long been seen as a problem for anthropology. *Totemism* is Levi-Strauss' attempt at a solution. The book rejects earlier theories of totemism which posited a religious or functionalist explanation for what was seen as a unitary phenomenon, and instead argues that the correspondences and relationships established by totemic systems are not functional or religious, but intellectual, analogical. Thus, Levi-Strauss breaks down the unitary category of 'totemism' and reconstitutes it as one aspect, one specific example of, a more general, indeed universal, human necessity to develop conceptual systems by means of forms of classification. *The Savage Mind* continues this process by using systems of totemic classification to demonstrate that the thought processes of 'primitive' peoples are no less scientific than those characteristic of modern western societies. The starting point of *The Savage Mind* lies in the refutation of the claims made by a number of writers - for example Frazer, Lévy-Bruhl, and indeed Sartre - that the systems of thought of non-western societies could be described as 'primitive', irrational, or illogical. On the contrary, Levi-Strauss argues, 'primitive' or mythical thought is no more or no less scientific than is our own. Both forms of thinking 'require the same sort of mental operations and they differ not so much in kind as in the different types of phenomena to which they are applied.'[2]

While a member of a 'primitive' society might group together onions, garlic, turnips, radishes, cabbages and mustard at an intuitive level, a western scientist might do so because each contains sulphur. Thus, whereas western scientific thought is concerned with the formal relations and characteristics of and between abstract entities, mythical thought - the 'science of the concrete' - deals more with the sensible qualities of concrete objects. Both systems are equally valid forms of acquiring knowledge, and while the 'science of the concrete' may be characteristic of 'primitive' societies, it is not a prior stage in the evolution of western scientific thought: 'there are two distinct modes of scientific thought. These are certainly not a function of different stages of development of the human mind but rather two strategic levels at which nature is accessible to scientific enquiry.'[3]

Levi-Strauss compares the processes characteristic of the science of the concrete to those of *bricolage*. The term does not translate exactly into English. The *bricoleur* falls somewhere between a craftsman and an odd job man: a person skilled in working with his hands, but one who, unlike the craftsman, does not possess a set of specialized tools, working instead with whatever is available.

> The 'bricoleur' is adept at performing a large number of diverse tasks; but, unlike the engineer, he does not subordinate each of them to the availability of raw materials and tools conceived and procured for the purpose of the project. His universe of instruments is closed and the rules of his game are always to make do with 'whatever is at hand'.[4]

Thus rather than constantly invent new tools/concepts for the production of objects/discourse, the practitioner of the science of the concrete, in much the same way as the *bricoleur*, has to work with limited resources, constantly refashioning old materials from a finite set to make do, putting them aside only to re-use them at a later date in somewhat different circumstances. Ideas, beliefs, elements of myths, etc. operate in this way in mythical thought:

> The significant images of myth, the materials of the bricoleur, are elements which can be defined by two criteria: they have *had a use*, as words in a piece of discourse which mythical thought 'detaches' in the same way as a bricoleur, in the course of repairing them, detaches the cogwheels of an old alarm clock; and *they can be used again* either for the same purpose or for a different one if they are at all diverted from their previous function.[5]

Thus, the myths of 'primitive' peoples are the result of the reshuffling of these 'odds and ends' of thought, the rearrangement of elements standing in different relations to each other in different places.

The activity that unites these modes of thought is the insistence on classification. As we have seen, although the mode of classification may differ between mythical and scientific thought, it is the existence of classification that is of most importance. 'Classifying, as opposed to not classifying, has a value of its own, whatever form the classification may take.'[6]

This is because classification imposes order and stability on the world . All thought, in this sense, is analogous: we impose order on the world by classifying objects in the natural and social environments in terms of perceived oppositions, contrasts, differences, etc., and this is a defining feature of human thought: 'The logical principle is always to be *able* to oppose (terms) . . . . *How* to oppose is an important but secondary consideration.'[7] The method of classification is always on the basis of observed contrasts and oppositions: 'all classification proceeds by pairs of contrasts: classification only ceases when it is no longer possible to establish oppositions.'[8]

While the terms of classification are purely conventional, the relations between the terms have a consistent character; they are categorized in terms of binary oppositions. The terms are grouped into pairs of opposites which are then related to other pairs to form systems of oppositions:

The existence of differentiating features is of much greater importance than their content. Once in evidence, they form a system which can be employed as a grid is to decipher a text, whose original unintelligibility gives it the appearance of an uninterrupted flow. The grid makes it possible to introduce divisions and contrasts, in other words the formal conditions necessary for a significant message to be conveyed.[9]

This gives us a means for understanding the use which Levi-Strauss makes of the nature/culture distinction. It is not only a means for identifying what is culture and what is nature. It is a way of grouping the oppositions which appear in culture as classificatory systems. Totemism presents a system for ordering the differences and oppositions that exist in the social world by using natural species to explain these differences. Totemism postulates a homology not between natural species and social groups but between 'natural distinctions and cultural distinctions.'[10]

The homology they evoke is not between social groups and natural species but between the differences which manifest themselves on the level of groups on the one hand and on that of species on the other. They are thus based on the postulate of a homology between *two systems of differences*, one of which occurs in nature and the other in culture.[11]

The differences and relationships between animal species therefore become a way of thinking about and expressing the differences between social groups. Thus, the resemblances between animal species and social groups are not literal but analogical: 'it is not the resemblances, but the differences, which resemble each other.'[12]

Earlier explanations of totemism, such as that put forward by Malinowski, who argued that certain animal species were chosen as totems for utilitarian or functional purposes, are therefore mistaken: systems of totemic classification have an intellectual, rather than a practical purpose, 'natural species are chosen not because they are "good to eat" but because they are "good to think"'.[13]

The customs and beliefs associated with totemism represent only one level of classification among many, whose functions are the same in each case. 'They are allied to other beliefs and practices, directly or indirectly linked to classificatory schemes which allow the natural and social universe to be grasped as an organised whole.'[14] The value of practices such as forms of totemic classification resides in the fact that

> they are codes suitable for conveying messages which can be transposed into other codes, and for expressing messages received by means of different codes in terms of their own system .... Far from being an autonomous institution definable by its intrinsic characteristic, totemism, or what is referred to as such, corresponds to certain modalities arbitrarily isolated from a formal system, the function of which is to guarantee the convertibility of ideas between different levels of social reality.[15]

Thus totemic classification, caste systems, and systems of food prohibitions, which had previously been seen as completely separate institutions, are transformations of the same basic mental structure, all formally analogous, differing only in their relative positions 'within a wide system of reference which operates by means of a pair of contrasts: between general and particular on the one hand, and nature and culture on the other.'[16]

Classification proceeds via the use of binary oppositions because this is ultimately how the brain is structured. The mind operates by perceiving contrasts, oppositions, and distinctions, and builds up these perceptions into structured sets. This basic structure of binary thinking is a fundamental feature of the human mind. It is, 'an original logic, a direct expression of the structure of the mind (and behind the mind, probably, of the brain).'[17]

Levi-Strauss derives the inspiration for his arguments from the theories of structural linguistics, laid down by Saussure in the early decades of this century, and developed by the Prague school of linguists, chiefly Jacobson and Troubetzskoy. Jacobson argued that all languages display certain universal features; they can be broken down into relations of binary opposition. The relations between phonemes are relations of binary opposition, and the dozen 'distinctive features' that underlie these phonemic oppositions are themselves constituted by a single binary opposition.[18]

> There is an inventory of simple relations common to all tongues of the world. Such relations pertain both to the early acquisitions of children's language and to the most stable properties in those types of aphasic regress which display a mirror picture of infant's development. This repertory may be exemplified in phonemics by such simple relations as compact/diffuse ... grave/acute and ... nasal/non-nasal.[19]

Structural linguistics can provide the inspiration for a knowledge of the object of anthropology, Levi-Strauss argues, because it has demonstrated that for the first time a social scientific discourse has provided a scientific knowledge of its object. Moreover, recourse to the techniques of structural linguistics is possible because the objects of both discourses are the products, or the effects, of the same structure - the workings of the unconscious.

> Among all social phenomena, language alone has thus far been studied in a manner which permits it to serve as the object of truly scientific analysis .... This results from modern researches into the problem of phonemics, which have reached beyond the superficial conscious and historical expression of linguistic phenomena to attain fundamental and objective realities consisting of systems of relations which are the products of unconscious thought processes.[20]

Furthermore, not only are they the products of the same structure, but the various phenomena studied by the respective discourses are themselves similar in structure: cultural phenomena and linguistic phenomena can be studied by the same methods and techniques of analysis because they are composed of the same elements. Thus the various cultural configurations that comprise the object of anthropological study, like those studied by linguistics, are composed of systems of differences, relations of exchange, etc. In effect, he argues, cultural systems and linguistic systems can be treated similarly, because culture is structured like language.

> all forms of social life are substantially of the same nature - that is . . . they consist of systems of behaviour that represent the projection, on the level of conscious and socialised thought, of universal laws which regulate the unconscious activities of the mind.[21]

> Like phonemes, kinship terms are elements of meaning; like phonemes, they acquire meaning only if they are integrated into systems. 'Kinship systems', like 'phonemic systems', are built by the mind on the level of unconscious thought . . . . Although they belong to *another order of reality* kinship phenomena are *of the same type* as linguistic phenomena.[22]

Levi-Strauss has been criticized both because of the use he makes of categories of binary opposition such as that between nature and culture and also because of the claims for universality that he has made for them. It has been argued that to transpose a set of categories designed for the analysis of one society on to all others is ethnocentric. Jack Goody, for example, in *The Domestication of the Savage Mind* has written of the opposition thus,

> This opposition has penetrated so deeply into cultural analyses that we regard it as 'natural', inevitable. However, the division between nature and culture is in some ways rather artificial . . . . If the dichotomy is not all that obvious in our own society . . . in many other cultures we find no corresponding pair of concepts . . . . I would claim that there is no such pair in either of the two African languages known personally to me (LoDagaa and Gonja). Though there is certain 'opposition' of 'bush' and 'house', 'cultivated' and 'uncultivated', there is nothing that would correspond to the

highly abstract and rather eighteenth century dichotomy that is current in western intellectual circles.[23]

Similarly, the collection of essays edited by MacCormack and Strathern, *Nature, Culture and Gender*, argues that the opposition is a particularity of western thought:

> there is ethnographic evidence to suggest that in the form in which Europeans now conceive it, the contrast is not a universal feature of consciously held folk models.[24]

> In selecting from our own repertoire of overlapping notions certain concepts envisaged in a dichotomous or oppositional relationship (nature vs. culture), we are at best making prior assumptions about the logic of the system under study, and at worst using symbols of our own as though they were signs.[25]

While this may be so, it does not refute Levi-Strauss's arguments. For the empirical criticisms miss the point. Levi-Strauss is not claiming that, at the level of conscious thought, all societies utilize a distinction between nature and culture; his arguments are not based at the level of everyday experience. He says, rather, and this is his main point, that the human brain classifies and categorizes experience and information according to a set of binary oppositions of which the distinction between nature and culture is but one example, and that this occurs on an unconscious level.

But why does the distinction between nature and culture have this privilege? This cannot really be answered at the level of empirical findings or unconscious processes. Its source in Levi-Strauss's thought really derives from his own distinction between nature and culture, his own myth, as it were, of the origin of culture. This is elaborated in the first chapter of the *Elementary Structures of Kinship* where he argues that all societies are founded upon a distinction between nature and culture through the universality of the prohibition of incest. This prohibition provides the means by which the opposition between nature and culture is transcended. While 'of no acceptable historical significance',[26] this distinction is nevertheless fundamental to social theory, to the extent that, 'to deny or to underestimate this opposition is to preclude all understanding of social phenomena.'[27]

Of what does this opposition consist? 'Nature' and 'culture' are seen as two distinct realms, both exhibiting unique qualities. Nature is characterized by universality, in the sense that everything happens in accordance with the laws of nature; culture by contrast is constituted by the existence of rules, which always take the form of particular systems of rules, systems which therefore differ from each other. These differences mean that cultures in so far as they are possible forms of Culture, differ from each other in a realm which exhibits particularity rather than universality. The problem of course is to think out the transition between the two - where nature ends and culture begins. This is why feral children have the same significance for Levi-Strauss as they had for the eighteenth century. He dismisses the documented cases of feral children as 'cultural monstrosities', congenital idiots who had been abandoned because of their idiocy, and who thus cannot furnish us with 'evidence of an earlier state'.[28] Similarly, the search for the point of transition at the other extreme, the possibility of the beginnings of a cultural level among the anthropoid apes is also dismissed. Apes, he claims, nowhere exhibit any regular patterns in their behaviour, any consistency in their social life that might allow for 'the formulation of any norm'. This last point is important, for it is the existence of rules that defines culture. Speaking of the behaviour of apes, Levi-Strauss writes,

> This absence of rules seems to provide the surest criterion for distinguishing a natural from a cultural process.
> The foregoing discussion has not merely brought us to this negative result, but has provided the most valid criterion or absence of rules in patterns of behaviour removed from instinctive determination. Wherever there are rules we know for certain that the cultural stage has been reached.[29]

Nature is characterized by universality, culture in terms of the presence of rule governed behaviour.

At this point Levi-Strauss introduces the problems posed by the prohibition of incest, the group of facts that constitutes a 'scandal' in terms of the ordering matrix of the nature/culture opposition, in that it possesses the main characteristics of both nature and culture in being both a rule and universal:

> We refer to that complex group of beliefs, customs, conditions and institutions described succinctly as the prohibition of incest, which presents, without the slightest

ambiguity, and inseparably combines, the two characteristics in which we recognise the conflicting features of two mutually exclusive orders. It constitutes a rule, but a rule which, alone among all the social rules, possesses at the same time a universal character.[30]

Here therefore is a phenomenon which has the distinctive characteristics both of nature and of its theoretical contradiction, culture. The prohibition of incest has the universality of bent and instinct, and the coercive character of law and institution.[31]

The prohibition represents a 'scandal' because it cannot find a place within the classificatory scheme established by Levi-Strauss. By exhibiting the characteristics of both nature and culture - being both universal and a rule - it falls outside the classification itself. It is universal, and therefore a part of nature, but is also cultural because it is a rule. There is no society, no social group that does not prohibit marriage between certain classes of relative, the exceptions being either temporary or limited to certain classes or groups in a population, such as the aristocracy or royalty. And although the prohibition varies somewhat in its field of application - some societies prohibit marriage with a sibling, some with a half-sibling, or a cousin - there are no societies in which some form of incest avoidance is not practised, 'there is no absolute exception'.[32]

Levi-Strauss criticizes the explanations of earlier writers like Morgan, Frazer, and Durkheim, who explained incest prohibitions either purely in terms of nature or of culture, or who posed an extrinsic connection between the two. Rather, he argues that the prohibition is neither natural nor cultural, nor a bit of each, but is the very bridge between the two, the moment by which the opposition between nature and culture is established.

The prohibition of incest is in origin neither purely cultural nor purely natural, nor is it a composite mixture of elements from both nature and culture. It is the fundamental step because of which, by which, but above all in which, the transition from nature to culture is accomplished . . . . Before it culture is still non-existent; with it, nature's sovereignty over man is ended . . . . It brings about and is in itself the advent of a new order.[33]

But the prohibition of incest is not solely a negative rule; by prohibiting it also prescribes. The incest taboo might be seen as a prohibition from within the proscribed circle, but viewed in terms of the culture it is a productive set of possibilities, rather than prohibitions. It is a positive rule in that it prescribes certain marriage partners and thus ensures the constant flow of women between social groups. The exchange of women strengthens the group by building up alliances with other groups; by compelling a man to marry outside his immediate group incest avoidance enables alliances to be established between groups - a woman is given with the expectation that one will be received in return. 'The biological group can no longer stand apart, and the bond of alliance with another family ensures the dominance of the social over the biological and of the cultural over the natural.'[34]

Incest avoidance and its corollary, exogamy, thus constitute 'the supreme rule of the gift', an example of the principle of reciprocity. In demanding that the members of the group marry outwards, the prohibition of incest avoids the possibility of contraction that incestuous marriages would involve. By the continuous circulation of women between groups, incest taboos increase solidarity, and ensure 'the existence of the group as a group.'[35] By controlling the distribution of women, one of the 'scarce products' of the group, incest avoidance constitutes an expression of 'collective intervention'.

> The prime role of culture is to ensure the group's existence as a group, and consequently, in this domain as in all others, to replace chance by organisation. The prohibition of incest is a certain form, and even highly varied forms, of intervention. But it is intervention over and above anything else; even more exactly, it is *the* intervention.[36]

Thus by prohibiting possible natural sexual relationships the taboo on incest constitutes the founding moment of culture. It is a necessary condition for society, the condition that allows for the very possibility of culture.

One problem with Levi-Strauss's account of this process is this category of a 'natural' sexuality that is denied expression by the operation of the incest taboo. Speaking of polygamy, he writes, 'Social and biological observation combine to suggest that, in man, these tendencies are natural and universal, and that only limitations born of the environment and culture are responsible for their suppression.'[37] Thus, for Levi-Strauss, culture - in the form of rules and punishment, the laws against incest - intervenes, and marshalls these 'natural' ('incest-inclining') sexual desires into acceptable channels, obeying marriage laws: exogamy and the exchange of women. Natural sexuality, therefore, still remains, but as an object regulated by culture.

Levi-Strauss's view of sexuality can be contrasted with that of Freud. Like Levi-Strauss, Freud accords a central importance to the incest taboo for the founding of society; however for Freud, the prohibition on incest affects the constitution of individuals' sexual identities, through the operation of the Oedipus complex. Moreover for Freud sexuality can never be simply reduced to a biological instinct defined in the traditional sense as genetically pre-determined behaviour that is common to all members of the same species, but is a product of the complex interplay of biological, social, and psychic factors. One of the problems with the English translation of Freud's work is that the word 'instinct' is used to render two German terms, instinct (*instinkte*), understood in the strictly biological sense, as above, and 'drive' (*Trieb*), denoting a form of somatic pressure directed to the release of tension: 'the use of "Trieb" accentuates not so much a precise goal as general orientation, and draws attention to the irresistible nature of the pressure rather than to the stability of its aim and object.'[38]

Freud understood sexuality to be a product of these drives, a more complex organization than the instincts, which, while having a somatic foundation are psychically constructed and determined. Thus Freud claimed that the sexual instinct lay 'on the frontiers between the mental and the physical'.[39] As Hirst and Woolley state,

> Freud remains within the field of the biological theory of instincts, although differentiated from it. Thus 'instincts' (drives) might be considered as a concept substituted for instinct (in the strict biological sense) in the analysis of an animal with higher psychological functions, *Homo sapiens.*[40]

Freud never understood sexuality or incestuous wishes as being simply a natural phenomenon, the result of a biological instinct, or an original attribute of the human species. This can be demonstrated with reference to the process of 'anaclisis'. His concept refers to the process by which the sexual instinct 'leans upon', or is 'propped up' by other bodily functions; the act of sucking at the mother's breast is an activity that is engaged in not simply for the need for food, its original or primary purpose, but soon becomes a means for providing a form of 'bonus pleasure'. Thus an activity associated with the instinct for self-preservation becomes the site of sexual pleasure, over and above its original function:

> The satisfaction of the erotogenic zone is associated, in the first instance, with the satisfaction of the need for nourishment.[41]

> To begin with, sexual activity attaches itself to one of the functions serving the purpose of self-preservation and does not become independent of them until later.[42]

Sexuality, then, attaches itself to, and finds its first source in, another instinct, and becomes an autonomous activity only as a secondary consequence of this attachment. As Hirst and Woolley state,

> Sexuality is *always* a derived form, there is no original or primal sexuality. Thus the auto-eroticism of the infant is not something it is born with, it is a development subsequent to an anaclitic constitution of the sexual instincts.[43]

Infantile sexuality, according to Freud, is bisexual, polymorphous, and perverse. The child is born with no fixed physical sexual identity, and the aim, object, and source of sexuality are not pre-given, possible combinations of all three can appear. The fixing of sexual identities is only achieved through the resolution of the Oedipus complex, a process that is not confined to a single route. Heterosexual genital sexuality is not given, it represents one possible form, not the only necessary one:

> psychoanalysis considers that a choice of an object independently of its sex - freedom to range equally over male and female objects . . . is the original basis from which, as a result of restriction in one direction or the other, both the normal and the inverted types develop. Thus . . . the exclusive sexual interest felt by men for women is also a problem that needs elucidating and is not a self-evident fact based upon an attraction that is ultimately of a chemical nature. A person's final sexual attitude is not decided until

after puberty and is the result of a number of factors, not all of which are yet known.[44]

Thus for Freud human sexuality cannot simply be reduced to biologically predetermined behaviour, but is over-determined by, and organized through, complex social and psychic forms. Indeed, it has been argued that in other primate species also, sexual behaviour is far more complex than this, and cannot be understood in terms of a simple reflex or instinctual model. Young male chimpanzees in particular, have to learn how to copulate: when placed with a receptive female in oestrus, sexually mature but inexperienced males often have difficulty in performing coitus. Ford and Beach claim that

> Adult monkeys and chimpanzees that have had no heterosexual experience often are unable to copulate with the oestrus female .... As far as the male chimpanzee is concerned, several months or even years of practice and experience in sexual performance appear essential to the development of maximal coital efficiency.[45]

Elsewhere, Beach argues that increasing cortical control over sexuality is an important feature of primate life, whereas in sub-primate mammals, sexuality is controlled by hormones secreted from the reproductive glands. He concludes,

> Heredity, as represented by the relatively stereotyped and inflexible functions or capacities of the subcortical neural mechanisms and the gonadal hormones, plays the major role in the courtship and mating of subprimate species. Environment or experience, as it effects the more modifiable cortical functions and the capacity of cortical activity to alter the responsiveness of lower centres, is of primary importance in the sexual behaviour of the higher mammals.[46]

Thus in both humans and chimpanzees, where cortical control is more marked and where instinctive responses operate to a far lesser degree, learning plays an important part in the development of sexual activity.

The aim of this chapter has been to demonstrate the place of the categories of nature and culture in the work of Claude Levi-Strauss.

We have seen how, in *The Savage Mind*, the opposition between nature and culture is crucial for the construction of the categories necessary for a science of the concrete, of the importance for 'primitive' thought of systems of totemic classification. We have also seen how in *The Elementary Structures of Kinship* the concepts operate as mutually exclusive and jointly exhaustive categories, how Levi-Strauss utilises the twin criteria of norm and universality for differentiating the social from the non-social, and how the incest taboo acts as a form of contract theory in making possible the transition from a state of nature to one of culture. What consequences follow from Levi-Strauss's use of the categories of nature and culture, and how important are they in his work? The categories are important for they underpin his understanding of culture as a self-enclosed realm of phenomena, an autonomous level of society rigidly differentiated from biological phenomena:

> Any culture can be considered as a totality of symbolic systems ... [which] seek to express certain aspects of physical reality and of social reality and, furthermore, the relations between these two types of reality and between the symbolic systems themselves.[47]

Here Levi-Strauss is continuing a line of thought characteristic of - although by no means exclusive to - the tradition of American cultural anthropology that was discussed in the previous chapter. Culture is specific to 'man', in fact, it is the possession of culture that marks off the human from the non-human:

> The concept of culture originated in England, since it was Tylor who first defined it as 'that complex whole which includes knowledge, belief, art, morals, law, custom, and any other capabilities and habits acquired by man as a member of society'. Culture therefore relates to the specific differences between man and animals, thus leading to what has ever since been the classic antithesis between *nature* and *culture*.[48]

Culture is specific to humanity because that is the only species that has a capacity for language, a phenomenon which along with the existence of rule-governed behaviour, defines culture: 'language is ... the prototype of the *cultural phenomenon*, (distinguishing man from the animals).'[49]

Of course there are immense differences between Levi-Strauss's structuralism and the procedures of American cultural anthropology. But my argument is that at a certain point they both employ the nature/culture distinction as a metaphysical device for grounding and distinguishing the human sciences. I have already detailed how this occurs in respect to Boas *et al*. In the case of Levi-Strauss it is more circuitous. The nature/culture distinction is first deployed as a means of grouping classification systems. In this sense it seems at first as if he is employing the distinction as a methodological tool. But in *The Elementary Structures of Kinship* this turns out to have an ontological foundation which requires him to treat sexuality and its incestuous 'wishes' as natural. A comparison with Freud, who of course makes the incest taboo central, none the less marks Freud's capacity to conceive of sexuality in a non-metaphysical way, that not as something which belongs to a special order of being, nature. This is the metaphysical thread which we have followed in order to demonstrate that Levi-Strauss depends upon the very distinction he is trying to draw.

3

Beyond the bounds of culture:
the noble savage
and the wild man

In the previous two chapters we saw how the oppositions between nature and culture, human and animal, have been used as a means for 'grounding' the human sciences, and we discussed some of the difficulties inherent in the forms of dualism associated with the use of such oppositions. But specifying the terms of these oppositions is not just a problem for the contemporary human sciences. For just as the distinctions between nature and culture, the human and the animal, have a long history in western thought, so too the problems involved in making those distinctions explicit have an equally long history. A discussion of the themes of primitivism and wildness, and of stories of feral children, serves to elaborate these problems. The main figures associated with these themes - the noble/ignoble savage, the wild man, the wolfchild - cannot easily be fitted into any of the above categories. Indeed they disrupt the terms of the oppositions, since they reside in the space between the natural and the cultural, the human and the animal. Throughout both classical antiquity and the Middle Ages there were no hard and fast criteria for establishing membership of the human species and attempts to mark out the boundary between the natural and the cultural were always fraught with difficulties. Even when, during the eighteenth century, it was deemed possible - through the use of systematic classification based on observation and analysis - to distinguish human from animal with scientific rigour, the criteria put forward to establish that distinction were still by no means clear. It is here that stories of wolf children, discussed increasingly during the eighteenth century, become important. For such children were seen as possible subjects of the 'crucial experiment', an experiment designed to establish the limits of humanity, to answer one of the central questions of the Enlightenment, What is 'Man'?

Interestingly, the debates in the contemporary human sciences concerning feral children rehearse the arguments and positions established in the earlier eighteenth century debates, where the existence, or not, of such children was used to support opposed and contradictory theories concerning the nature of human behaviour and capacities. In some respects, little has changed: for while feral children are no longer seen as a test case for the radical sensationalism of Locke and Condillac, in their discussions of these cases contemporary social scientists continue to make use of oppositions between nature and culture, and human and animal in order to defend their claims as to the uniqueness of human culture. As the following discussions demonstrate, there are no - nor have there ever been any - simple ways of demarcating the natural from the cultural, no clear cut means by which the capacities and attributes of human beings can be marked off as being in some way essentially different from those of other animals.

We begin with a discussion of primitivism. The theme of primitivism, and its corollary, the 'noble' savage, are related to a long tradition of myth and poetry which goes back to the beginnings of written history. Descriptions of foreign peoples as noble savages, living a happier and more virtuous life beyond the bounds of civilization appear in the writings of both Homer and Herodotus. The beliefs and attitudes associated with primitivism, however, comprise a complex set of ideas rather than a clear body of thought. In *Primitivism and Related Ideas in Antiquity* Boas and Lovejoy distinguish two main forms: chronological and cultural primitivism. The former is, as the name suggests, associated with the belief that the period of greatest happiness for humanity occurred at the beginning of history, a period which no longer obtains. It is a kind of philosophy of history, generally involving a theory of the Fall, but a philosophy that can take various forms depending upon the particular characterization of the time process of history. It is with cultural primitivism, however, that we will be mainly concerned. This represents, according to Boas and Lovejoy,

the discontent of the civilized with civilization, or with some conspicuous and characteristic feature of it. It is the belief of men living in a relatively highly evolved and complex cultural condition that a life far simpler and less sophisticated in some or in all respects is a more desirable life.[1]

51

Cultural primitivism can often be combined with chronological primitivism, as when the people seen by the primitivist as the exemplars of a more simple and virtuous life are represented as having existed at some earlier stage in human history. Generally though this is not the case; the model for cultural primitivism is most usually found in the present, 'in the mode of life of existing primitive, or so-called "savage" peoples.'[2]

There are two different forms of description characteristic of cultural primitivism which concern the conditions of life of the peoples about whom the primitivist enthuses, which we may call 'soft' and 'hard' primitivism. Descriptions of life characteristic of 'soft' primitivism depict the savages as creatures of leisure. Free from the pernicious ties and constraints of civilization, they live in harmony with nature, freely expressing their impulses and emotions untrammelled by social rules and regulations. Never wanting for food, which is always plentiful, they live their lives in a state of idleness and self-indulgence.

The life of 'hard' primitives, on the other hand, is characterized by a high degree of physical hardship. Theirs is a spartan existence with few, if any, of the cultural and material trappings of civilization. Always on guard against predatory animals, and usually in a harsh, unfavourable climate with barren soil, the 'hard' primitives eke out a meagre existence in a constant war against nature.

Throughout antiquity descriptions in terms of 'soft' primitivism were applied almost exclusively to the imaginary races that were thought to live on the edges of the known world: the Hyperboreans, Ethiopians, etc. Although, as Boas and Lovejoy point out, in the case of the Ethiopians this was an idealization of an actual race, the descriptions owed more to the mythic imagination than to any known reality. The designation 'hard' primitive on the other hand, was reserved for those races actually known to the primitivists of the ancient world - the Scythians, and the various Germanic tribes - who were to become the model for the figure of the noble savage towards the end of the classical period. The Stoics and Cynics were chiefly responsible for this, for, as the main promoters of primitivistic thought on the ancient world they praised those aspects of the savage life which, as they saw it, were living examples of their own philosophy.

The distinction between 'hard' and 'soft' primitivism is a significant one; its importance becomes most marked with the return of primitivistic ideas and the reappearance of the figure of the noble savage to Europe during the seventeenth and eighteenth centuries, particularly in the wake of the voyages of Cook and Bougainville to the South Seas. For here the ideas and beliefs associated with 'soft' and 'hard' primitivism directly influenced the attitudes of Europeans towards the native peoples of the South Pacific.

The image of people living in a state of nature comprises several aspects, many of which - sometimes all - are often found together. The phrase 'state of nature' itself is a composite of a number of specific states of nature which are found, again often together, in classical literature. The most important of these are the 'technological state of nature': an existence without most of the arts or cultural attributes of civilized life, and the 'economic state of nature': society without private property, a form of primitive communism. Invariably though, the term will include a 'juristic state of nature': society without government, and also a 'dietetic state of nature': vegetarianism. The latter form is particularly common; reference is often made in ancient literature to the 'milk drinkers of the north', and savage races who live on a diet of fish, milk, herbs, and berries. Indeed vegetarianism seems to have remained a popular element in the composition of such figures; mediaeval texts relating to the mythical 'wild man' often remark upon this. Homer, in the *Iliad*, refers to the land of 'the noble mare-milkers and the milk-drinking Abioi, the most righteous of men.'[3] The references to the Abioi as 'just' also seems to be fairly common; elsewhere in the *Iliad* Homer refers to them as being 'supremely upright'. Other savage peoples are often portrayed as being just and noble; for example, the Chauci, one of the Germanic tribes described by Tacitus in the *Germania*:

They are the noblest people of Germany, and one that prefers to maintain its greatness by righteous dealing. Untouched by greed or lawless ambition, they dwell in quiet seclusion, never provoking a war, never robbing or plundering their neighbours.[4]

The practice of describing the Ethopians as if they were one of the imaginary races living at the edge of the world originated, according to Volckler, with Homer:

The Ethiopians are with Homer a general name for the last inhabitants of the earth, the most remote people he knew of.

The epithet 'blameless' rests perhaps on grounds similar to those on which certain Scythians are elsewhere denominated the most just among men (the Abioi), viz., a confused notion of the innocence and justice of semi-savage nations that are but little known.[5]

If Homer's account of the Ethiopians in the *Iliad* is tempered with 'soft' primitivism, then Tacitus' descriptions of the lives of some of the German tribes in the *Germania* is a classic example of 'hard' cultural primitivism. Every aspect of life, from the state of the climate, to the various marriage laws, are described in glowing terms of 'hard' primitivism. Of the countryside Tacitus asks

Who would have been likely to leave Asia Minor, North Africa, or Italy, to go to Germany with its forbidding landscapes and unpleasant climate - a country that is thankless to till and dismal to behold for anyone who was not born and bred there?[6]

However, the Germans have been 'inured' by living in such a harsh climate 'to cold spells and by the poverty of their soil to hunger', which is perhaps fortunate, because the countryside in general 'is covered either by bristling forests or by foul swamps.'[7]

Describing family life, Tacitus writes of their child-rearing practices thus: 'In every home the children go naked and dirty, and develop that strength of limb and tall stature which excite our admiration. . . . The young master is not distinguished from the slave by any pampering in his upbringing.'[8] Their diet is discussed in similar terms: 'Their food is plain - wild fruit, fresh game, and curdled milk. They satisfy their hunger without any elaborate cuisine or appetisers.'[9]

Of all the 'savage' races known to the ancients the Scythians were without doubt the most commonly described in the language of 'hard' cultural primitivism, they were the noble savages *par excellence* of the classical world, in much the same way as the Amerindians were to become for the primitivists of the sixteenth and seventeenth centuries. This tradition of depicting the Scythians as noble savages persisted into the early Christian period. Hugo of Saint Victor wrote of them:

Accustomed to wander through untilled spaces, the Scythians do not cultivate their fields, but convey their wives and children with them in wagons, protected from the rain and the severity of winter by hides. And they drive their flocks and herds along with them. . . . They live on milk and honey, a people strong in work and in war, of huge corporeal strength.[10]

Clement of Alexandria uses similar language:

Of the heathens, the Celts and the Scythians wear their hair long, but they do not embellish it. . . . Both these barbarian tribes hate luxury. The Germans will summon as a clear witness to this the River Rhine, the Scythian will summon his wagon. Sometimes the Scythian makes light even of his wagon. . . and abandoning luxury, he leads a simple life. The Scythian takes his horse, a sufficient home and less cumbersome than his wagon, and mounting it, is borne wherever he wishes.[11]

Both of these descriptions are examples of pagan cultural primitivism, as of course are all the examples from classical antiquity. For the early Christians, however, the idealization of 'savages' constituted a problem, one which, for obvious reasons, did not exist for pagans; for not only were they not Christian - and, moreover, held responsible for the martyrdom of the early evangelists - but any notion of a pure and natural life, of a fundamental goodness unrelated to the divine doctrine of life in the Garden of Eden, could only conflict with established religious authority. Thus, in the writings of early Christian Latin authors, descriptions reminiscent of cultural primitivism are replaced increasingly by a conception of savages as bestial, cannibalistic creatures, and it is this anti-primitivist tradition of the cruel, rather than the noble, savage which predominates in early medieval literature. The end of the ancient world sees also the eclipse of primitivistic thought. From the early Middle Ages, for a period of over one thousand years, primitivism was to lie largely dormant, reappearing again in Europe in the sixteenth and seventeenth centuries. Nevertheless, contrasting views of savagery continued to exist throughout the Middle Ages, views which both originated in classical writings. As Boas states, 'The use of the savages as evidence either of nobility or baseness kept alive the various traditions of their customs which had been influential in classical Greek thought and which were to reappear later in the Renaissance.'[12]

The primitivism that developed within the Christian tradition imagined the inhabitants of distant lands, (generally earthly paradises located in the East, full of precious stones, rare metals, etc.) as being pure and living by nature in accordance with God. This type of quasi-primitivism, combining simplicity and luxuriousness, although very different from that of the cultural primitivism discussed earlier, is closely related to another tradition stemming from the ancient Greeks.

This tradition is itself comprised of a set of contradictory images, and is in turn partly derived from the epics of classical Indian mythology, depicting the existence of fabulous and monstrous races living in the east, predominately in India itself: the 'marvels of the East'. Rudolph Wittkower[13] has shown that works from within this tradition were responsible for the western conception of India for almost two thousand years. The earliest important text was written at the beginning of the fourth century BC by Ktesias from Knidos, a physician at the court of Artaxerxes Mnemon of Persia. In this work Ktesias included tales of people with a single large foot, the sciapodes; cynophalia, the men with dog's heads who could not speak but who barked; headless people with their faces between their shoulders; giants, and men with tails.

The next text of any importance appeared towards the end of the fourth century BC. It was written by Megasthenes, an ambassador to the court of the Indian King Sandracottus, at the end of Alexander the Great's campaigns in India. Megasthenes repeated the old stories found in Ktesias, and added some of his own, of serpents with wings like bats, huge winged scorpions, etc. This work remained unchallenged as the most authoritative text on India for nearly fifteen hundred years. After the second century BC direct traffic with India was disrupted, and the literary tradition was insulated from the experience of travellers. Thus, up until and including the early Middle Ages, western knowledge of India was based mainly on the works of Ktesias and Megasthenes.

These stories and legends concerning India were handed down to the early medieval period via writers like Pliny and Solinus, who both accepted uncritically the older accounts of the Greeks. But the 'marvels' were not just found in written treatises; there was a large pictorial tradition handed down from antiquity. The 'marvels' also appeared as illustrations in cosmographies, romances, maps, etc., and could be found in the work of such scholars as Albertus Magnus and Roger Bacon and other encyclopedias of the twelfth and thirteenth centuries.

Thus the classical tradition of depicting fabulous races of men and monsters on the Indian sub-continent becomes fused with a form of Christian quasi-primitivism. Two good examples of this, both literary works which enjoyed great popularity and which appeared in many editions throughout the Middle Ages, are the 'Alexander romance' and the story of Prester John. Both of these contain many of the Indian fables from the 'marvels of the East' legends. The 'Alexander romance', translated from the Greek in the early Middle Ages, was the imaginary story (though regarded as real history throughout the Middle Ages, and attributed to Callisthenes, a historian on Alexander's campaigns) of Alexander the Great's meeting with a non-Christian people (the Brahmins, who replaced the Scythians, as far as Christians were concerned, as the model noble savages) living an essentially Christian life in India.

The story of Prester John concerns an imaginary letter, supposedly written by a fabulously wealthy, but Christian, king (Prester John) to the Byzantine emperor Manuel Comnenus in the mid-twelth century, which included along with a description of the wealth and power of Prester John's kingdom - seen as an earthly paradise - a check-list of the ubiquitous 'marvels'. The link between paradise and India is a long established one, dating from the book of Genesis. Indeed Columbus, on his voyage to America, was certain that he passed close by it.

Although the 'marvels of the East' tradition was instrumental in keeping alive the view of savages as noble, virtuous, or innocent, it was, however, at the same time the source for later writers in the early Middle Ages such as Solinus and Isidore, who took the opposite view, portraying savages as bestial and monstrous etc. Both Solinus, in *De Mirabilibus Mundi* (ADc.170), and Isidore of Seville, in his *Etymologies* (622-3), reproduced the stories, contained in the older accounts, of the fabulous races of classical antiquity - giants, dog-faced men, cyclops, satyrs, pygmies, cannibal Scythians, etc. Isidore writes of the Scythians thus: 'Some of these people cultivate the land; some monstrous and savage, live on human flesh and blood.'[14]

These views persisted throughout the Middle Ages and the Renaissance, and were given wide currency in the travel literature and travel fiction that developed as a result of the voyages of geographical discovery beginning towards the end of the thirteenth century. Accounts of the early voyages, from the Dominican and Franciscan monks of the thirteenth century, to Columbus, Marco

Polo, and Magellan, were a curious amalgam of fact and fantasy, where unicorns and satyrs rubbed shoulders with apes and monkeys. Indeed, the 'marvels' survived well into the seventeenth century in the illustrated cosmographies already mentioned. The father and sons DeBrys, who were engravers by trade, published between 1590 and 1635 cosmographies of the newly-discovered America and East Indies, which they illustrated as a way of displaying their skills. Their illustrations included the familiar two-headed monsters, sea-cows with horns, unicorns, etc. - many of the fabulous creatures characteristic of the Middle Ages. This, however, should not be taken simply as evidence of medieval naïvety. As Wittkower has argued,

> Many of the travellers were learned; they had a knowledge of classic authors, they knew their Christian encyclopaedias, their treatises on natural science, their romances, they had seen on their maps the wondrous nations in those parts of the world to which they were travelling - in short, their imagination was fed from childhood with stories of marvels and miracles which they found because they believed in them.[15]

Similarly, in *The Order of Things* Michel Foucault argues forcefully that there was no great inconsistency between description based on accurate observation and the acceptance of stories and legends passed down from ancient writers. And this is not to be explained by the gullibility of Renaissance thinkers and their susceptibility to superstition. Rather, it is the result of a different way of ordering knowledge. Until the second half of the seventeenth century, Foucault argues, knowledge of a plant or animal was based not only upon observed properties accurately described, but included everything that had been said or written about it - commentaries from ancient authors, fables and legends, uses to which it could be put, etc. Foucault writes,

> The division, so evident to us, between what we see, what others have observed and handed down, and what others imagine or naïvely believe, the great tripartition, apparently so simple and so immediate, into *Observation, Document* and *Fable*, did not exist. And this was not because science was hesitating between a rational vocation and the vast weight of naïve tradition, but for the much more precise and much more

58

constraining reason that signs were then part of things themselves, whereas in the seventeenth century they become modes of representation.[16]

To reiterate, then, the general argument being advanced here: as the discussions of primitivism and anti-primitivism have shown, marking out the boundaries between nature and culture, and between human and animal was no easy matter in the classical and early Christian periods. Both 'noble' and 'ignoble' savages existed alongside unicorns, satyrs, Scythians, Ethiopians, giants, and members of other fabulous and monstrous races. A further demonstration of these difficulties can be shown by way of two discussions: first, how the Middle Ages attempted to account for savages; and second, by examining the mythological figure of the wild man.

For the Middle Ages the problem of savagery involved the issue of how to classify members of savage races, and this meant where to place them in the hierarchy of being, a complex chain of existence linking every living being in a unity of gradations. The notion of the world as a 'great chain of being' is a conception of the universe that was generally accepted from the early Middle Ages to the late eighteenth century. It can most easily be described as a combination of two strands of classical philosophical thought: the Aristotelian principle of continuity, and what A.O. Lovejoy has called the principle of plenitude. The former, which occurs in Aristotle's writings on natural history, argues for a shading off of one class of being into the next, without clear-cut distinctions between them. The principle of plenitude, which Lovejoy attributes originally to Plato, represents the belief that all things that could exist should and do exist; it is what Lovejoy calls 'the "fullness" of the realisation of conceptual possibility in actuality'.[17]

> From the Platonic principle of plenitude the principle of continuity could be directly deduced. If there is between two given natural species a theoretically possible intermediate type, that type must be realised - and so on *ad infinitum*; otherwise, there would be gaps in the universe, the creation would not be as 'full' as it might be.[18]

Together, these two principles result in a conception of the universe as a continuous chain of existence, a great chain of being composed of an immense, or - by the strict but seldom rigorously applied logic of the principle of continuity - of an infinite number of links ranging in hierarchical order from the meagrest kind of existents, which barely escape non-existence, through 'every possible' grade . . . up to the highest possible kind of creature.[19]

The elimination of even one link, would lead to chaos; 'ceasing to be "full", the world would cease to be in any way "coherent"'.[20]

In the hierarchical scale of beings humans occupied an intermediate position, a middle link in the chain between beast and angel, material and spiritual. Thus the great chain of being functioned as the major means for ordering and classifying the multitude of forms that existed, from the sentient to the intellectual, that testified to the great diversity of the creator's handiwork. Since every being had its logical and correct place in the great scheme of things the issue was where to place the savage. According to Margaret Hodgen, in *Early Anthropology in the Sixteenth and Seventeenth Centuries* (1964), there were three possibilities; the savage could be accepted as fully human and classified alongside other Europeans; he could be regarded as something less than a European, and classified accordingly in a secondary human category; lastly, the savage could be ranked among the animals, seen perhaps as the highest animal. For orthodox Christians, argues Hodgen, the issue did not constitute a problem; adherence to the doctrines contained in the scriptures determined that savages were human, however bestial or degenerate in their behaviour. According to some interpretations of the biblical texts, however, savages, though they might be considered human, were clearly regarded as inferior to civilized Europeans - civilization, of course, being equated with Christianity. Indeed, in a declaration made in 1537, Pope Paul II claimed that while the Amerindians could be considered human, their acceptance into the human race was conditional upon their conversion to Christianity. Or again, savages could be described, as they sometimes were by the early travellers, in terms of the myriad hybrid creatures of classical antiquity; satyrs, centaurs, dog-headed men, etc. As Hodgen writes of the travellers,

Bred from childhood on the ethnical fables of Pliny, Solinus and company, they found it easy to mistake what they saw for what they had been told by these fabulists. When confronted with the Red Indian, painted and befeathered, or with the

Hottentot, naked and dirty, it seemed only reasonable to see in these specimens the kind of abnormal ethnological phenomena they had been led to expect, especially on the margins of the world.[21]

And she notes that Sir Walter Ralegh, 'reported the existence of semi-human beings or half-men, fit only for a place below man himself in the hierarchy.'[22]

In the thirteenth century the encyclopedist Albertus Magnus included these *similtudines homines* in his hierarchical scale of creatures. His book *De Animalibus*, contains an individual description of every species, but concentrates on humanity and its relationship to the rest of the animal world. Albertus Magnus, unlike most writers recognized three categories: humans; human-like creatures, such as pygmies, apes, etc; and other animals. This category of *similitudines homines* is probably the earliest example of a 'missing link', an attempt to bridge the gap between humans and animals. One example of these *similitudines homines*, for Albertus, was the pygmy. He believed in their existence - in the Middle Ages pygmies were included among the list of fabulous races that made up the 'marvels of the East' - but not that they were human. As John Burke writes,

> In his view they were wild, in a state midway between man and the ape. To illustrate his point, Albert related one of the first of many stories concerning mental defectives or other unfortunates found in the state of nature apart from but close to civilisation. His tale concerned a wild couple who were tracked by hunters and attacked by their dogs. The woman did not survive the ordeal, but the man was cornered and captured. Thereafter, Albert wrote, the man was taught to stand erect but could learn only a few words and obviously did not possess reason. Pygmies, in Albert's view were similar to such wild men.[23]

After Albertus Magnus these questions lay dormant for nearly four hundred years. Philosophical speculations concerning the possible existence of forms linking humans to animals lower in the chain of being did not gain wide acceptance until the seventeenth century.

Just as the contradictory images of the 'noble' and 'ignoble' or bestial savage developed in parallel throughout the pre- and early Christian periods, there emerged during the Middle Ages a figure in which these two opposing images became combined in one unstable complex: the mythological wild man. If the noble/ignoble savage is a representative of a distinct race of beings, the wild man - or, to a much lesser extent the wild woman - is almost always a solitary figure, living, if not completely alone, then only with a mate. Although wild man myths have existed since pre-Christian times it was in the Middle Ages that the figure came to prominence, and indeed overshadowed his more romantic counterpart the noble savage. To trace precisely how and when this occurred is beyond the scope of this work. However by the end of the sixteenth century this process is reversed and the noble savage re-emerged as something of a cult figure. As Richard Bernheimer in *Wild Men in the Middle Ages* states,

> To gauge the influence of the literature on the noble savage upon the interpretation of the wild man in the Middle Ages is not easy, since as a figment of native thought the wild man almost always lacks at least two of the attributes of his classical counterpart: his pacifism and his vegetarianism. . . . We will have to go as far as the sixteenth century before again coming upon such a clear example of native mythology moulded in the form of the noble savage of antiquity, for in the intervening period the wild man reigned supreme.[24]

The wild man, a figure composed of human and animal qualities, hirsute and usually lacking language, appears in the art and literature of the Middle Ages as a survival from pre-Christian times. Most of the literary material on the wild man dates from the twelfth century and after; the earliest representations in art are from the mid-thirteenth century, and the period of his greatest popularity was the latter half of the fourteenth century. It is important to note, however, that the wild man is not just a literary figure, but also the subject of popular beliefs - which could still be found in some parts of central and southern Europe well into the nineteenth century.

So it should not be thought that the wild man simply disappeared at the end of the Middle Ages. The issues and themes associated with this complex figure, and indeed some of his characteristics, were later to become crucial in the controversy surrounding feral children. As Dudley and Novack remark,

> This mythic being, reared by wolves or bears, living in isolation, possessed of enormous physical strength and sexual

potency, covered with hair and often without language, survived the realities of the voyages of discovery and lived on not only in the western psyche, but also in its official taxonomy as developed by Linnaeus.[25]

The wild man represented an important trend in medieval thought, occurring in the writings of Cervantes and Spenser, the paintings of Albrecht Dürer and Pieter Bruegel, and on various artefacts of everyday life, such as candlesticks, drinking-cups, caskets, etc. Richard Bernheimer outlines the two views of wildness and the wild man: on the one hand he is portrayed as a brutal and savage creature, cunning and ruthless, and possessing an uncontrollable and insatiable sexuality. On the other, he is a benign and proud figure; primitive and unrestrained, but benevolent and sympathetic, a child of nature. Both of these themes place the wild man beyond the bounds of human culture. In the first he is the antithesis of all social life, a creature to be feared and hated. In the second, as with the earlier noble savage, wildness is seen as freedom, as an escape from the constraints of civilization. Fear and terror give way to admiration and respect; the wild man becomes an innocent of the pure life.

By examining the linguistic origins of the names associated with the wild man Bernheimer suggests a possible genealogy for these themes:

> Philological evidence thus endows the wild folk with a dual nature, depicting them as demons of the fertile earth and at the same time as ghosts from the underworld. To the wild man Silvanus, benefactor of fields and woods, there corresponds the wild man Orcus, enemy of living things and of man himself.... It was the synthesis of the two conflicting interpretations which made possible the mythology of the wild folk: on the side of life their care for the animals and their readiness to make their advice available to the human community; and on the side of death their appalling ugliness, cannibalism, frightful temper.[26]

That both of these themes were present together in the image of the wild man should not be surprising; for - as in the case of savagery discussed earlier, the place which the figure occupied in the thought of the Middle Ages was by no means consistent. Medieval authors openly contradicted one another in attempting to assess the wild man's status. Often, unable to unravel the theological complexities involved in interpreting the scriptures, writers conceived of the wild man in sociological and psychological terms. Human beings were reduced to a state of wildness by some misfortune, an upbringing among animals, or insanity. As Hayden White remarks,

> The wild man (or woman) was generally believed to be an instance of human regression to an animal state . . . wildness is what a normal human being takes on as a result of losing his humanity, not something possessed as a positive force, as the power of the devil was.[27]

Indeed, the terms wildness and madness were used almost interchangeably throughout the Middle Ages. Neither necessarily specified a permanent state; wildness was not seen as being irreversible, but as a condition which was amenable to change through acculturation - as with madness, which was often held to be a periodic state, and not at all continuous and permanent. A good example of this in much late medieval literature is the relationship between wild men and knights. The latter could often be found suffering from periodic bouts of 'love madness', caused by some all-consuming desire. The afflicted knight would then live the solitary life of a wild man, in the woods, until his passion subsided. Indeed, the wild man was often in competition with a knight for a lady's affections, as Bernheimer shows with illustrations of thirteenth and fourteenth century love caskets, and, in some cases, would often be the successful suitor:

> Having been a wild man is no impediment to a knightly career, once the defects, appurtenant to the wild state have been removed. Indeed if we are to believe some authors of the fifteenth and sixteenth centuries, the limits between wildness and knighthood were fluid, and to become a gentleman the wild man did not have to shed much of his savagery.[28]

The wild man could even be held up as an example of integrity and responsibility:

> The very fact that a man was brought up in the woods may confer upon him a certain incorruptible quality, which alone enables him to resist temptations to which others succumb, and thus to attain aims inaccessible to them.[29]

Different attitudes towards the wild man existed side by side during the medieval period: attitudes which ranged from fear and hostility, to curiosity and amusement, and ultimately respect and admiration. Towards the end of the Middle Ages the image of the wild man was modified, his more benevolent side gradually came to predominate over his negative qualities and the figure was transformed back into the noble savage. This process took place between the fifteenth and seventeenth centuries, and coincided with the age of geographical discovery. This was no coincidence, for one of the effects of the voyages of discovery was to bring Europeans into contact with, and give them a greater knowledge and understanding of, other cultures. Europeans looked to these other cultures in order to better understand their own. The wild man/noble savage came to symbolise these other cultures, and became a source for a movement of cultural relativism that developed and which was to have profound implications for European social and political thought.

4
Feral children:
the debate on the
limits to humanity

The travel literature and fiction that developed as a result of the voyages of geographical discovery caught the imagination of the European reading public and resulted in the re-emergence of primitivistic ideas and of the noble savage as a figure of importance. During the sixteenth century this reawakened interest in primitivism was intensified by the development of a new genre of travel literature which involved accounts of both real and imagined voyages. Much of this literature goes under the name of the 'extraordinary voyage'. This was the term given to a type of novel that developed in French literature at the end of the sixteenth and beginning of the seventeenth centuries. The 'extraordinary voyage' was

> a fictitious narrative purporting to be the veritable account of a real voyage made by one or more Europeans to an existent but little known country - or to several such countries - together with a description of the happy conditions of society there found and a supplementary account of the travellers return to Europe.[1]

This genre, which was characterized by its realistic exotic setting in far-off lands, developed as a result of increasing interest in newly discovered cultures, as reported in accounts of voyages actually made. Apart from works of pure imagination, the 'extraordinary voyage' novels contained a high degree of geographical 'realism'. This was most marked in works written after 1675 when authors used detailed accounts of real voyages, as opposed to the earlier accounts which relied mostly on an imaginary realism. This later realism was made even more striking by the use of detailed maps

66

(even if grossly inaccurate) and meticulous descriptions of birds, animals, plants, and fruits, so that 'the far lands became in some measure real to those who stayed at home.'[2]

The figure of the noble savage was used, via the travel literature, in much the same way as its classical counterpart: as a vehicle for criticizing, in the form of satires, the morals and customs of contemporary European society. Frequently, mythical utopias were used to serve as a model for Europe, and here the geographical realism became important. As Atkinson in *The 'Extraordinary Voyage' in French Literature* notes, 'It is precisely by the authenticated realism of their setting that the "extraordinary voyages" carried weight as works of religious, social, or political criticism.'[3]

This use of the novel form for the purposes of social criticism was particularly marked in its attitude to the church; many of the books contained reports of distant lands enjoying peace and plenty without churches and priests. In general, the social, political, and religious institutions of Europe fared badly by the comparison; the most important of these works, Fénelon's *Telemaque* (1699), which remained popular with young people throughout the eighteenth century, was in fact a political and moral critique of the government of Louis XIV.

From the middle of the seventeenth century the work of French Jesuit missionaries spawned a new type of travel literature. The missionaries, working mainly in Canada, and to a lesser extent, Paraguay and China, published regular 'relations' on their work with the native Indians, in which the latter were described in the glowing terms of cultural primitivism. As Symcox has observed, 'Jesuit theology encouraged the adoption of an optimistic view of human nature and led the missionaries to paint a favourable - not to say rosy - picture of the natives of Canada.'[4]

This resulted in the Canadian Indians becoming the model for the noble savage. The missionaries saw them as examples of 'uncorrupted virtue and innate nobility', living without many of the vices associated with a civilized existence. The Indians 'thus became representative figures of simple virtue, superior in every way to Europeans save in their ignorance of revelation, and this defect would soon be made good by the labours of the missionaries.'[5]

In France, certainly, the idealized representation of the Huron which was to grace the pages of the philosophical treatises of the eighteenth century was already a popular image before the end of the seventeenth century. The resurgence of interest in primitivism reached its zenith by the middle of the eighteenth century, and coincided with the expeditions to the islands of the South Pacific and Australasia. Bernard Smith, in *European Vision and the South Pacific*, notes that the first Europeans to visit the South Pacific tended to see its inhabitants in terms of the tradition of primitivistic thought.

> European observers sought to come to grips with the realities of the Pacific by interpreting them in familiar terms. Both classical antiquity and the traditions of Christian thought provided a stock of attitudes and preconceptions which Europeans continually brought to bear upon their experience of the Pacific.[6]

As in the classical world, both 'hard' and 'soft' primitivism were very much in evidence: the inhabitants of Tahiti were seen essentially as 'soft' primitives, whereas the Fuegians, the Maoris, and the Tasmanian Aborigines were usually described in the terms of 'hard' primitivism. The island of Tahiti was described as being like Paradise before the Fall, and its inhabitants as living in a natural state of innocence. Not all aspects of Tahitian life, however, were seen in this light: infanticide, prostitution, symbols of paganism, 'licentious dances', etc., all served to outrage European public opinion. This was especially the case during the last decades of the eighteenth century, when the increasing influence and importance of evangelical thought did much to spread the idea that the lives of the savages, rather than being innocent and virtuous, were depraved and could only lead to sloth and degeneration. As it happens, the wrath of the established church was confined principally to the values of 'soft' primitivism: 'the notions of austerity and fortitude associated with hard primitivism being somewhat more congenial both to Calvinistic Christianity and to the romantic interest in the historical origins of the Northern nations of Europe.'[7] In France, particularly, the ideas and values associated with the Revolution brought the virtues of 'hard' primitivism back into favour. 'Simple in his needs and desires, self-disciplined, courageous, and with a great capacity for endurance, the savage became a symbol of revolutionary freedom and ideal perfectibility.'[8]

Smith shows how the accounts of the voyages provided the satirists of the eighteenth century with a wealth of material. The islands of the South Pacific, and their inhabitants, became the basis for a flood of satires on, and moral critiques of, the institutions of European society, especially its religious ones. Perhaps the most famous of the latter is Diderot's *Supplement au Voyage de Bougainville*, written in 1772. In the *Supplement* Diderot extols the virtues of the lives of the Tahitians, describing them in the now familiar terms of 'soft' primitivism, and holding them up as a model to be followed, in contrast to the corrupt and immoral state of European society.

The later voyages, those of Cook and Bougainville, for example, were undertaken in a much more scientific spirit than the earlier ones, and served to stimulate interest in natural history, geology, and meteorology, and the emerging discipline of anthropology. This concern with scientificity was a result of the increasing importance of classification. Between 1735 and 1758 the taxonomist Linnaeus published ten editions of his *Systema Naturae*, an attempt to classify in one systematic table all living beings. Such was his influence, that his work 'in the classification of plants and animals was extended to the classification of clouds by meteorologists and the classification of climates by geographers.'[9]

Like all taxonomists of the seventeenth and eighteenth centuries Linnaeus attempted to relate his findings to the great chain of being. The expeditions to the South Pacific returned with a large number of new species of flora and fauna, birds, fruit, etc., which began to undermine this conception of the universe. The increasing demand for these new varieties of plant and animal life led to a much more rigorous approach to the methods of observation and collection, and these methods were beginning to be applied in turn to the study of humanity. Ironically, the voyages that had done so much to popularize the theme of primitivism and the figure of the noble savage, were responsible for their subsequent decline. Although the early exploration gave some credence to the view that the Pacific islands represented a 'golden age', the increase in information concerning the natural history of the Pacific peoples contributed to the eventual acceptance of the idea of evolution, in much the same way as the numerous new varieties of plant and animal life discovered in the Pacific discredited the old system of classification based on the theory of the great chain of being. Increasing contact with, and knowledge of, non-western cultures, then, was gradually beginning to undermine the basis for the beliefs and attitudes associated with primitivism. The view that humanity had degenerated after an initial state of perfection was slowly being questioned, and replaced with early notions of progress, and of the evolution of society out of an original state of savagery. In other words, the primitivistic view of humanity as being in a state of progressive decline was giving way to early notions of evolution.

According to A.O. Lovejoy, this change can be shown in the work of Rousseau. It has become a commonplace to see Rousseau as the father of the noble savage, as one of the leading champions of primitivism. Lovejoy suggests, however, that to see him simply in these terms is misleading, and ignores an important theme in his work. Rousseau's treatise on the original condition of mankind, the *Discourse on the Origins of Inequality*, should rather be seen as an early form of 'sociological evolutionism', which is the logical opposite of primitivism. Lovejoy admits that Rousseau does 'waver between two conflicting tendencies'; although influenced by the tradition of primitivistic thought, he was 'working himself free from it', and moving away from a position of seeing humanity as descending from a state of primitive perfection, to one in which it had ascended from a state of animality, through the gradual unfolding of an attribute which Rousseau, following Diderot, called 'perfectibility'.[10]

This interest in early notions of evolutionism led to speculation that the original condition of the European races might be similar to that of present day 'savage' peoples. If so, then the study of the customs, languages, etc., of 'savages' might reveal something about the origins of humanity. As Symcox notes,

> Information about non-European cultures was treated more rigorously in an attempt to throw light on the whole question of the origins of society. It was felt that the Noble Savage was the key to understanding the motives which had originally led men to form their social groupings. What was needed, therefore, was more precise information about the true condition of the Savage. In other words, anthropological data were to be used to solve the historical problem of the origin and development of cultures.[11]

The concern with the search for the origins of society must be seen in the context of a wider interest in the question of origins in general, an interest which was extended to include the origins of music and the arts, of culture, and of the nature of humanity itself - the origins of language and of human knowledge. These questions, then, were bound up with a desire to understand the natural history of humanity. This interest in the question of origins was not purely, or even primarily, concerned with gaining knowledge of the primeval condition of humanity, but was an attempt to separate what was innate in man from what was artificial or secondary, to mark off nature from culture, to distinguish human from animal. As Hirst and Woolley have argued, it was with the rise of classification and natural history in the eighteenth century that the problem of determining what is, and what is not, a 'man' became a crucial issue. With the birth of the human sciences and the appearance of 'man' as a distinct object of knowledge, the category of the 'human' comes to denote a specific set of attributes and capacities - capacities specifiable by recourse to the procedures of empirical science. The importance given over to determining the nature of humanity makes the drawing of the boundary between nature and culture, and human and animal a scientific exercise. So the categories nature/culture, and human/animal become distinctions grounded in empirical science.

> The question of the boundary becomes decisive, even if observational knowledge remains uncertain. In 1758, when Linnaeus published the *Systema Naturae*, the 'known world' had almost as many gaps as in Pliny's day - a great deal of Africa and Asia remained unexplored. Linnaeus' classification differs from ours and includes *Homo troglodytes* as a distinct variety of the human species and also includes the 'orang outang' (*sic*). But the issue is not whether the boundary is correctly drawn, rather that it is held to be drawable. The progress of knowledge and observation would make the classification exact and exhaustive.[12]

And the key was observation. Rousseau's state of nature, Condillac's speechless statue, and the wild couple, were all popular examples of the attempt to reconstruct the natural endowments of humanity - but they were all hypothetical. The emphasis placed upon observation and experimentation meant that the search for an understanding of the limits of humanity had to be directed elsewhere. As contact with non-western peoples increased it became clear, owing both to an understanding of the effects of colonisation, and a growing awareness of acculturation, that 'savages' could no longer be seen as examples of natural, uncorrupted humanity. The 'noble savage', however useful as an example of the relativity of cultural practices or as a figure with which to criticise European morality, was not a living embodiment of 'natural man'.

For a truly experimental study of 'man' two possibilities presented themselves, both of which became the subjects of extensive philosophical debates towards the end of the eighteenth century. First, the discovery of the anthropoid apes, whose resemblance to humans had always attracted discussion; and second feral children: children who, although possessing the potential for social life, had been excluded from it. Travellers returning to Europe from Asia and Africa brought with them both chimpanzees and orang-utans, and the apes' obvious human-like qualities sparked off a controversy as to the exact nature of their relationship to man. The issue came to a head when Linnaeus, in his *Systema Naturae*, classified 'man' as a quadruped and placed humanity in the same order as apes: anthropomorpha. The debate, however, was already under way at the very end of the seventeenth century. In 1699 the anatomist Edward Tyson published *Orang-Outang, sive Homo Sylvestris, or the Anatomy of a Pygmie compared with that of a Monkey, an Ape, and a Man*. The book was in fact the result of his dissection of a young chimpanzee, and not an orang utan, a year earlier. Tyson was familiar with Jacob Bontius's *Historiare Naturalis* (1658) which contained a description of an orang-utan, and which was, in Robert Wokler's words, 'perhaps the first European reference to the orang-utan of South-East Asia, despite the fact that the artist's impression of this creature portrays only a pilous woman with a shaggy mane like that of a lion.'[13]

In fact, this description owed more to the long tradition of wild man myths than to any accurate observation of the animal. Indeed, the name 'Orang-utan' comes from the Malaysian word for 'wild man'. According to Wokler, Tyson saw his work as providing a comparison between the orang-utan's body and the human body, and also as providing a solution to the mysteries of the ancient mythological figures of the satyr, cynocephalus, etc., by claiming that they were all species of ape. Though as Janson points out, by virtue of calling the orang-utan both a 'pygmie' and *Homo sylvestris*, Tyson allowed the non-technical reader to presume that it was essentially human. Janson notes that this occurred at a time when travellers were returning from Africa with tales of the Hottentots, a race of 'savages' seemingly more bestial than human.

Thus we need not be surprised that the eighteenth century found it difficult to distinguish the Orang-utan, the 'super ape' whose physical and mental resemblance to man was believed to go far beyond the limits of a mere animal, and the lowest forms of man such as the Hottentots, who failed to live up to the accepted minimum standard for human beings.[14]

Linnaeus gave credence to the view that orang-utans might be a race of wild men by classifying them as a species of man, *Homo nocturnus*, in his *Systema Naturae* in 1736. Certainly Rousseau and Monboddo both speculated that the orang-utan might be more advanced than many 'savages'; in Monboddo's case this was rather more than speculation: he claimed that the animal walked erect and was capable of using a stick for attack and defence.

A number of commentators suggested that the orang-utan might be the 'missing link' in the great chain of being between man and the apes. As Lovejoy notes,

This preoccupation with the question of man's relation to the anthropoids gave an especial 'philosophical' interest to the rather numerous descriptions of the Hottentots by late seventeenth and early eighteenth century voyagers. They were probably the 'lowest' savage race thus far known; and more than one writer of the period saw in them a connecting link between the anthropoids and *Homo sapiens*.[15]

Tyson himself acknowledged his support for the chain of being, declaring his aim to exhibit the scale of nature, in which the orang-utan appeared 'the nexus of the animal and rational'.[16] The essential difference, he claimed, was that the orang-utan lacked the reason of the human mind. Here Tyson is expressing the Cartesian doctrine that animals were sentient beings lacking both a soul and reason. This was, of course, one of the traditional criteria for distinguishing humans from animals. It did not go unchallenged, however. Monboddo claimed not only that orang-utans were rational beings, but that they and humans were of the same species: orang-utans were a part of the human race that had failed to develop; they lacked the quality of 'perfectibility', the gradual unfolding of the higher intellectual faculties that had evolved in humans.

Monboddo's reasons for making this claim were perfectly in line with the knowledge of comparative anatomy of his day:

as to his body, he [the orang-utan] is altogether man, both outside and inside, excepting some small variations, such as cannot make a specific difference between the two animals, and I am persuaded are less considerable than are to be found betwixt individuals that are undoubtedly of the human species.[17]

Monboddo saw as another indication of the animal's intelligence its use of a stick as a weapon for attack and defence 'which no animal merely brute is known to do.'[18] Hans Aarsleff, however, suggests that Monboddo based this claim on illustrations of apes seen walking with a stick, a conventional detail of late fifteenth century iconography of the primate. According to Aarsleff the stick was introduced in about 1486 because it would have offended religious doctrine to show an ape walking erect, a feature taken to be the exclusive privilege of humans so that they could lift their heads towards the heavens and be aware of the divinity.[19]

Rousseau, too, was prepared to speculate that perhaps these 'men', 'that have tails like quadrupeds', were members of the human species. Discussing travellers' tales about such beings he mentions the possible effects of the diversity of climate, air, and food. He continues,

All these observations . . . make me wonder whether various animals similar to men, taken by travellers for beasts. . . . would not in fact be true savage men whose race . . . had not had an opportunity to develop any of its potential faculties, had not acquired any degree of perfection, and was still found in the primitive state of nature.[20]

He argued that the differences between these creatures and men were less than those between one man and another, and suggests that the reason why travellers classified them as beasts and not men was to do with 'their stupidity and also because they did not talk'. Such reasons, Rousseau declared, were in themselves inadequate, for although the organs of speech were natural to humans, speech itself was not, being a product of their perfectibility.

Rousseau and Monboddo were not the only ones to suggest that there might be a close affinity between the orang-utan and humanity, or indeed whether the orang-utan was a member of a savage race of men living in the state of nature. The various travellers' tales and accounts of these strange creatures were becoming increasingly common and commanded a wide measure of respect. Maupertuis, the president of the Berlin Academy of Sciences, wrote in 1768,

> It is in the islands of that sea [the Pacific] that voyagers assure us they have seen wild men covered with hair and having tails, a species halfway between ourselves and the monkeys. I would rather spend an hour in conversation with one of them than with the greatest *bel esprit* in Europe.[21]

Language, of course, was the most important criterion used to distinguish between humans and animals. On this Descartes had written,

> Of all the arguments that persuade us that animals are without thought, the key one is that, although animals have the ability to express their affections, never to this moment have we seen any animal arrive at the point of perfection of using a true language, that is to say, of expressing, either by voice or gesture, something which can be related to thought only and not to natural impulse. Language is in effect the sole sure sign of latent thought in the body; all men use it, even those who are dull or deranged, who are missing a tongue, or who lack the voice organs, but no animal can use it, and this is why it is permissible to take language as the true difference between man and beast.[22]

Although Descartes was probably regarded as the most authoritative voice on the matter, a number of arguments were put forward against his position. One, associated principally with La Mettrie, was the thesis that language was in need of no metaphysical principles of the soul to explain it, and that orang-utans, like humans, may be taught to speak. Indeed, in 1751 La Mettrie suggested that this might be easier than trying to teach language to deaf children. Another argument is associated with Rousseau and Condillac, and is the objection that in the natural state the language of humans differs very little from that of orang-utans. It is due to the attribute of perfectibility that humans are able to develop language. A third argument, associated with Monboddo, is the philosophical objection that language is not a necessary sign of either thought or humanity, and therefore that orang-utans can be just as rational as humans. Language, for

Monboddo - as for Rousseau and Condillac - is not natural to humanity, but is a product of its perfectibility, for 'not only solitary savages, but a whole nation, if I may call them so, have been found without the use of speech.... This is the case of the orang-Outangs.'[23] Besides, reasoned Monboddo, if persons born deaf have been taught to speak why not orang-utans? After all, they are possessed of a human intelligence; perhaps their lack of language is a consequence of the - as yet - non-appearance of the faculty of perfectibility.

It has already been noted that a preoccupation with the origin of language was a common feature of the eighteenth century. Indeed, from the 1740s onwards the question of language origins enjoyed an immense popularity and provoked a wealth of discussion and written treatises. In France, La Mettrie, Condillac, and Rousseau all published work on the subject; in England Horne Tooke and Lord Monboddo; and in Germany, Maupertuis, Herder, and Hamann. As we have seen, such a preoccupation had implications that were not merely linguistic, but that dealt with the question of origins in general. As Hans Aarsleff has remarked,

> Since the possession of language and speech has always been considered as the chief characteristic of the human species, the question of its origin has also been considered fundamental in any attempt to understand the nature of man and what distinguishes him from other animals.[24]

We have seen how the voyage of discovery helped to stimulate and kindle an interest in the origins of human societies, and of culture, and how important these developments were for the emergence of anthropology. We have seen, too, the interest shown in relation to the anthropoid apes and in questions concerning their relationship to humanity. It is, therefore, hardly surprising that an interest in these questions should draw attention to stories of wolf children reportedly found living a solitary life in the wild, isolated from any human contact. Given the controversy caused by the orang-utan's resemblance to man, it was little wonder that the discovery of such children became such a *cause célébre* for eighteenth century philosophy: it was rumoured that they were covered in hair, walked only on all fours, and were without language, that they shunned human contact, preferring instead the company of animals, and indeed behaved more like animals than human beings; it was not surprising that they were seen as the possible subjects for the 'crucial experiment', an experiment designed to lay bare the essential characteristics of human nature, to distinguish between the natural and the cultural - in effect to try and answer the question: what is the nature of man? Stories of wild children had been discussed with increasing interest throughout the eighteenth century. Indeed in 1726 one such child, Peter of Hanover, was brought to London, where Dr Arbuthnot attempted, apparently unsuccessfully, to educate him.[25] Linnaeus, who in the *Systema Naturae* classified wild children as a separate sub-species, *Homo ferus* (and as quadruped, mute, and hirsute) mentions nine examples, and discussions of these cases appeared frequently in the writings of Rousseau, Condillac, Herder, Buffon, and Monboddo. But it was the discovery of a boy aged about twelve found living in the forests of southern central France in January 1800, that was to provide the philosophers with the surest means for establishing the criteria for membership of the human species. Or so it seemed.

Victor, the 'wild boy of Aveyron', was discovered near the village of Saint-Sernin in the district of Aveyron, in southern central France, in early January 1800. He was first seen in 1797, and in the subsequent three years was captured twice, albeit briefly, in 1797 and 1798, only to escape into the surrounding forest, where he was sometimes seen by local villagers. When captured, the boy had no language, walked upright with difficulty, appeared deaf - indeed all his senses at first seemed dulled; he was impervious to heat and cold, unable to focus his attention on any one thing for any length of time.

After a brief period in a local orphanage the boy was taken to Paris and placed in the charge of the Society of Observers of Man. The Observers of Man was a somewhat shortlived philosophical society dedicated to investigating the 'natural history of man'. It drew its inspiration from the ideologues, chiefly from the sensationalist philosophy of Condillac. The society, which numbered amongst its members the leading intellectuals and scientists of the day, set up a committee to examine Victor. The group was headed by Philippe Pinel, one of the country's leading doctors, who was later to become famous as one of the founders of modern psychiatry. Other members included the anatomist Cuvier; the linguist Sicard; Jauffret, the secretary; and the anthropologist de Gérando. Pinel examined the boy and concluded that he was a congenital idiot, and therefore ineducable, and that that was the most likely reason for his abandonment. Jean Itard, a young surgeon at the Institute for Deaf Mutes in Paris - where Victor had been lodged, and whose director, the Abbé Sicard, was one of the founder members of the Observers of Man - dissented from the views of his superiors, and secured permission to attempt to educate the boy. Though they were both followers of Condillac, Itard took the contrary view to Pinel, believing instead that Victor's behaviour was a consequence of the long period he had spent in isolation, and not the result of some congenital deficiency. It was perhaps understandable that Pinel had diagnosed Victor an idiot, for his view, as expressed in his recently published *Treatise on Insanity* was that idiots were 'destitute of speech or confined to the utterance of some inarticulate sounds. Their looks are without animation; their senses stupified; and their motions heavy and mechanical.'[26] In the absense of evidence to the contrary the child should be classified as an idiot, he reasoned. Certainly, there appeared more grounds for a diagnosis of idiocy than for the speculative claims that the boy was a wolf child: there were no examples of wolf children to compare him with, whereas his behaviour fitted perfectly with that of other idiots. Indeed, in his first report on Victor, Itard himself had described the boy on his arrival in Paris thus:

a disgusting, slovenly boy, affected with spasmodic, and frequently with convulsive motions, continually balancing himself like some of the animals in the menagerie, biting and scratching those who contradicted him, expressing no kind of affection for those who attended upon him; and, in short, indifferent to everybody, and paying no regard to anything.[27]

For Itard, however, the boy was the living embodiment of Condillac's epistemology. He wrote,

If it was proposed to resolve the following metaphysical problem, viz. 'to determine what would be the degree of understanding, and the nature of the ideas of a youth, who, deprived, from his infancy, of all education, should have lived entirely separated from individuals of his species'; I am strangely deceived, or the solution of the problem would give to this individual an understanding connected only with a small number of his wants, and deprived, by his insulated condition, of all those simple and complex ideas which we receive from education, and which are combined in our minds in so many different ways, by means only of our knowledge

of signs. Well, the moral picture of this youth would be that
of the Savage of Aveyron, and the solution of the problem
would give the measure and cause of his intellectual state.[28]

Victor was to be a test case for the philosophy of radical
empiricism. Empiricism stresses the role of sensory experience in
the development of human knowledge. For such an epistemology,
the existence of humans deprived of the conditions necessary for
the normal development of those senses was clearly seen as
providing the means for the 'crucial experiment'. Just as Condillac,
in the *Traité des Sensations* brought his statue to life by endowing
it, one by one, with the five senses, so too would he, Itard, develop
a teaching programme designed to stimulate the boy's senses, and
to lead him to a development of the higher intellectual processes
dependent upon language.

It was through giving priority to the role of language in the
development of knowledge that Condillac radicalized and extended
Lockean empiricism. Language, for Locke, allowed for the
communication of general ideas between individuals. For
Condillac, however, ideas themselves were the result of a process
of association requiring the use of signs. Condillac thus reversed
the priority Locke accorded ideas over signs. As James Stam has
argued,

> Locke did not recognize the deeper epistemological relevance
> of signs, or of language generally, because he saw the main
> purpose of language in the communication of already formed
> ideas and overlooked its role in the very process whereby
> such ideas are formed.[29]

For Condillac, signs are necessary in order for man to reason: the
distinguishing characteristic of humanity is its ability to reason and
to form complex ideas, but it can only do so through the use of
signs. The use of signs makes possible the connection of ideas,
which for Condillac is the single principle to which all knowledge
can be reduced. In the *Essay on the Origin of Human Knowledge* he
writes,

> good sense, wit, reason and their contraries equally result
> from the same principle, which is the connection of ideas one
> with the other; and that tracing things still higher, we see that
> this connection is produced by the use of signs.[30]

So the main thrust of Itard's project was to teach Victor to speak, and he devised a programme designed to mirror Condillac's method of the development of knowledge. Victor's education lasted five years, and although his progress in other respects was considerable, the boy never learned to speak, and in the conclusion to his report on the experiment Itard remained ambivalent. It must be said, however, that although he considered the project only a partial success Itard none the less held to his original view that Victor's apparent 'idiocy' was of a functional variety, occasioned by his prolonged period of isolation. The only means by which Victor should be judged, he argued, was to compare the boy with what he was like when discovered:

> Beside a youth of the same age, he is only an unfortunate creature, an outcast of nature and of society. But within the simple comparison of Victor as he was and Victor as he is, one cannot but marvel at the vast gulf which lies between them and indeed there is more difference between our present Victor and the Wild Boy of Aveyron than between the same boy and other individuals of his present age and kind.[31]

Rather than being an ineducable idiot, oblivious to everything and everyone, save for the satisfactions of his immediate needs, Victor 'is capable of an affectionate friendship, is responsive to the pleasures of doing well, is ashamed of his mistakes and repentant of his outbursts.'[32] As to Victor's inability to acquire language, Itard claimed that this too was a result of his isolation, and that, as an adolescent, he was perhaps too old to be trained in its use.

The case of Victor has been discussed repeatedly by social scientists since the original disagreement between Itard and Pinel, and the issues continue to be relevant today. Indeed, the positions established in the debate find an echo in disputes concerning contemporary writers. Thus, Pinel's claim that Victor was an idiot (a claim supported by such writers as Gall, Spurzheim, and Esquirol) has been taken up by the anthropologist Claude Levi-Strauss, who, in his book The *Elementary Structures of Kinship* argues that all examples of wolfchildren were congenital defectives who were abandoned because of their idiocy. However, Lucien Malson in *Wolf Children*, and Harlan Lane in *The Wild Boy of Aveyron* reaffirm Itard's radical environmentalism. Malson, moreover, offers the case of Victor, and other examples of wolf children, as 'proof' that there is no such thing as 'human nature', that there are no human instincts. To these, a third approach can be added, that of the American child psychologist Bruno Bettelheim. In *The Empty Fortress* Bettelheim argues that wolf children are in fact suffering from a form of childhood psychosis: autism. Ironically, Bettelheim's manner of diagnosis, though not of course his conclusion, has some resemblance to that of Pinel. Both arrived at their conclusions on the basis of observed similarities between Victor and other children, diagnosed either as idiots or as autistic. And both approaches are open to similar criticisms. One is that similar effects can be produced by different causes; thus, there is often a confusion between correlation and causal explanation. Even if some of Victor's behaviour was like that of declared idiots or autists - and both of these conditions are not without diagnostic problems, even today - this would not prove that either idiocy or autism was the cause of the boy's condition, any more than saying that a high temperature was the cause of pneumonia. Victor spent at least two or three years, possibly more, living alone in the wild; the chances of an autistic - or mentally retarded - child surviving alone for that length of time are extremely small. And what of the other examples of wolf children? Zingg[33] has recorded over three dozen documented cases of extreme isolation; again, it seems unlikely that every one was suffering from either congenital brain damage or autism.

The case of Genie is interesting in this respect, and suggests caution in jumping to the conclusion of idiocy or autism as explanations of the behaviour of feral children. Genie was discovered in California in 1970, aged thirteen. She had been kept in conditions of extreme isolation (and abused and neglected) by a violent and severely disturbed father and an almost blind mother for twelve years. When found, her appearance bore more than a passing resemblance to that of other examples of severely isolated children. Susan Curtiss described her as follows:

> Genie was pitiful. Hardly ever having worn clothing, she did not react to temperature, heat or cold. Never having eaten solid food, Genie did not know how to chew, and had great difficulty in swallowing. Having been strapped down and left sitting on a potty chair, she could not stand erect, could not straighten her arms or legs, could not run, hop, jump, or climb; in fact, she could only walk with difficulty. . . . Having been beaten for making noise, she had learned to suppress almost all vocalization save a whimper. . . . She was

incontinent of feces and urine. . . . Genie was unsocialised, primitive, hardly human.[34]

Like Victor, Genie was seen as a test case; not, of course, for empiricist philosophy, but for a theory proposed by psychologist Eric Lenneberg claiming the existence of a 'critical period' for the acquisition of language. According to Lenneberg, language is a function of brain maturation and develops from 'mere exposure' to a linguistic environment between the ages of two and puberty. Before the age of two years language acquisition is not possible because the brain is not sufficiently mature, and after puberty normal language acquisition is not possible because the brain has matured and cerebral plasticity is lost. Having emerged at the age of thirteen after almost no linguistic input Genie, like Victor before her, was seen as the possible subject for the twentieth century's version of the 'crucial experiment'. By 1977, after more than six years of intensive teaching programmes, Genie had acquired a very limited degree of language use. From medical records available prior to her period of isolation, there is no evidence to suggest that Genie was suffering from any form of congenital deficiency, or displaying any symptoms of autism.

Stories of wolf children, like that of Victor, have been used by social scientists to support conflicting views with respect to questions about nature and nurture, environment and heredity. But, both in the original disagreement between Itard and Pinel, and in the contemporary debates, there is no simple opposition between environmentalists and hereditarians. As we have seen, Bruno Bettelheim is at pains to dismiss Victor as an authentic example of a feral child, substituting instead his diagnosis of autism. Bettelheim's desire to find such a solution to the problem of wolf children is understandable - a desire to ground the explanation in terms of medical science. In this way the solution can be located in the medical history of the individual; the study of wolf children is an (individual) problem for medical science, and not one for the human sciences.

Embedded in certain theories of behaviourism and social anthropology is the wish . . . to see man as wholly created by society. If infants raised by wolves were to become, to all intents, wolves, then we would have to accept that man is nothing but the product of his surroundings and associations.

It would seem that there are no inborn functions, no potentials that can either be developed or not by the circumstances of life, but never altered entirely.[35]

Bettelheim argues against this, claiming that 'no known society has ever done more than to modify innate characteristics.'[36]

The extreme reluctance on the part of social scientists like Bettelheim to accept the possible existence of feral children testifies to the importance of maintaining the oppositions between nature and culture and human and animal that such children would threaten. On the other hand, culturalists and behaviourists like Malson and Lane, with their view that human behaviour is infinitely malleable, are only too ready to admit of such a possibility, and to go to the opposite extreme, one that sees humans as being almost entirely the product of cultural influences - a *tabula rasa* - and that denies any importance to biological or psychological factors in the determination of human behaviour. Both sides use examples of feral children to support dogmatic positions which reveal, despite their differences, a similar underlying essentialism with respect to the categories of the human and of culture. The questions posed by examples of feral children can never be satisfactorily answered while the debates are set up in terms of radical distinctions between nature and culture, and human and animal. What the discussion of those debates reveals is the metaphysical dualism inherent in the use of such oppositions.

5

From Plato to Washoe:
talking apes?

Language is no longer the exclusive domain of man.
Penny Patterson (1978)[1]

The claims on behalf of ape language abilities are at best
unsubstantiated, and quite probably false.
Seidenberg and Petitto (1978)[2]

The previous chapter discussed some of the problems in eighteenth
century attempts to mark off the boundaries between nature and
culture, the human and the animal, and suggested that the continuity
between eighteenth century and modern debates on wolf children
results from a desire to maintain an essentialist distinction between
nature and culture. In this chapter I will attempt to show that these
problems have refused to go away and that the contemporary
human sciences continue to be embroiled in dogmatic disputes
about human uniqueness. The main focus will be on attempts to
teach chimpanzees a human sign language. The aim in reviewing
these experiments will be to show how a commitment to a
qualitative distinction between nature and culture and human and
animal underlies many of the theoretical positions in the debates
that have evolved. It will be argued that the main question at issue
in these debates - to what extent can apes use human language -
rests upon an outdated metaphysic, an anthropocentric
evolutionism that uses humanity as the yardstick by which to
measure the rest of the animal world. The real value of these
experiments lies in what they reveal about the nature of chimpanzee
intelligence and what continuities exist across the primate order -
to what extent the chimpanzee's ability to use a type of linguistic
symbol demonstrates the existence of significant similarities
between the human brain and the brain of the ape.

As we saw in the last chapter, language has always been seen as a defining characteristic of the human species, one of the attributes that most radically differentiates humans from other animals. For Descartes language represented 'the true difference between man and beast'. Descartes' dualism effected an a priori distinction between humans as rational beings, on the one hand, and animals as unthinking automata without the power of speech, on the other. The reason that animals lack language is not that they lack the necessary anatomical features or organs;

> For one sees that magpies and parrots can utter words as we do, and yet cannot speak as we do, that is to say, by showing that what they are saying is the expression of thought; whereas men, born deaf and dumb, deprived as much as, or more than, the animals of the organs which in others serve for speech, habitually invent for themselves certain signs, by means of which they make themselves understood by those who . . . have the time to learn their language. And this shows not only that animals have less reason than men, but that they have none at all; for we see that very little of it is required in order to be able to speak.[3]

Thus, animals do not use language because they lack reason.

But arguments claiming that language is an attribute unique to the human species are of course not confined to the seventeenth century: commenting on a paper written by the linguist Georges Mounin on the subject of ape-language experiments, Philip Lieberman has noted that 'the philosophic framework of the eighteenth century that makes language a unique, defining "human" attribute still unfortunately pervades linguistic theory. Humans have "language", animals "communicate".'[4] And another linguist, Dell Hymes, echoes these remarks: 'a preconceived commitment to "man's uniqueness in matters of language" seems to me a striking feature of contemporary anthropology and linguistics. The difference between "man" and man's primate kin is held to be radical, categorical.'[5]

Perhaps the most important and best known exponent of these views amongst contemporary linguists is Noam Chomsky. Chomsky argues that no other animal can use language because only the human brain has wired into its neural mechanisms the structures necessary to produce and comprehend it. Only humans are biologically predisposed towards language; no amount of training would result in apes, or any other animal, being able to acquire it. The discovery in other animals of a faculty 'closely analogous to the human language capacity ... would constitute a kind of biological miracle.'[6] On the question of the linguistic abilities of apes Chomsky is adamant; 'all normal human beings acquire language, whereas acquisition of even its barest rudiments is quite beyond the capacities of an otherwise intelligent ape - a fact that was emphasized, quite correctly, in Cartesian philosophy.'[7]

It should not be thought, however, that such views are restricted to linguists or cultural anthropologists. Consider the following, by a physical anthropologist who has written extensively on apes:

> The first point about animal society is an absolutely crucial one. It is that animals (by this I here mean all species other than man) do not think conceptually; they respond to stimuli or configurations of stimuli coming from within their own bodies and from the surrounding environment, but do not conceptualize either themselves, or others, or the external world and its parts, or their social group. The reason is that animals other than man lack symbolic-language systems needed to produce the cognitive constructions that are necessary for symbolic concept formation.[8]

The prevailing consensus, it seems, is that language is uniquely human. But there has always been a body of scientific opinion that has dissented from this view. We have seen that during the eighteenth century there was much speculation on the relationship between the anthropoid apes and human beings, and on the apes' cognitive and linguistic potential. Indeed, La Mettrie, in his *L'Homme Machine* suggested teaching sign language to apes, confident that they would be able to acquire it:

> Why should the education of monkeys be impossible? Why might not the monkey, by dint of great pains, at least imitate after the manner of deaf mutes, the motions necessary for pronunciation? ... it would surprise me if speech were absolutely impossible in the ape.[9]

La Mettrie's view was echoed nearly two hundred years later by the primatologist Robert Yerkes. Writing in the 1920s Yerkes argued,

I am inclined to conclude from the various evidences that the great apes have plenty to talk about, but no gift for the use of sounds to represent individual, as contrasted to racial, feelings or ideas. Perhaps they can be taught to use their fingers, somewhat as does the deaf and dumb person, and helped to acquire a simple, nonvocal sign language.[10]

Although the first sign language experiments with apes did not begin until the 1960s, more than forty years after Yerkes was writing, attempts to teach apes spoken language had been taking place since the turn of the century. One of the earliest was the effort of William Furness, an American doctor and explorer, to teach a young orang-utan to speak. Speculating on the possibility of 'civilising' the ape Furness wrote:

I was possessed with the idea that with constant human companionship and surroundings at an early age, these anthropoid apes - the orang-utan (which of course you know is a Malay name meaning Wildman or Man of the Jungle) - were capable of being developed to a grade of human understanding perhaps only a step below the level of the most primitive of human beings inhabiting the island.[11]

Moreover, he declared,

If deaf, dumb and blind children have been taught by beings they could not see to use language they could not hear would one not be justified in an earnest endeavour to teach the higher apes with facilities and senses alert and with traditional powers of imitation to do the same to a limited degree? It seems well nigh incredible that in animals so close to us physically that there should not be a rudimentary speech centre in the brain which only needed development.[12]

Furness returned to the United States in the autumn of 1909 with an orang-utan and a chimpanzee and embarked upon a laborious teaching programme. By the time he published his findings in 1916, however, he was forced to admit that his attempts had been singularly disappointing. The orang-utan, which had died two years previously, had after intensive and constant training learned two words, 'papa' and 'cup' (though this in itself was an achievement, for whereas human speech is produced while exhaling, the vocal cries of apes are produced whilst inhaling. Consequently, the ape was trying to speak whilst it was breathing in). The chimpanzee's attempts were also unsuccessful; after five years it had barely managed 'mama'.

The intellectual milieu within which Furness worked managed to accommodate a number of contradictory and mutually exclusive theories: Darwin's evolutionary theory, social Darwinism, and non-Darwinian Lamarckianism all coexisted together. More than forty years after the publication of *The Origin of Species* scientists and intellectuals were making pronouncements that owed more to a *scala naturae*, with humans at the top of the ladder, than to evolutionary theory. Much of this thinking characterized the approach of people like Furness, who argued that through a process of intensive education it might be possible to 'civilize' the ape somewhat, to raise it from its lowly station upwards in the direction of humanity. As Adrian Desmond remarks, '"Improvability" was the key, but that implied human standards and a predetermined goal. Man was again sitting on the Lamarckian apex of creation.'[13]

Around the time that Furness was conducting his experiment two other theoretical movements, both of which in very different ways were to influence the later ape language projects, were gaining adherents. Behaviourism and cultural determinism, although both committed to a strong environmentalist philosophy, were in other respects diametrically opposed to each other. Behaviourism rests on the belief that all animal behaviour, human included, is the result of complex processes of conditioning, responses to a variety of stimuli. Clearly, such a position would lend support to any attempts to teach language to other species. If language is not an attribute unique to the human species, a capacity for which only humans are genetically predisposed, but merely a form of verbal behaviour, then given the correct stimulation and reinforcement techniques, any animal could be trained in its use. Cultural determinism, on the other hand, admits of no such possibility. We saw in chapter 1 that for Kroeber it is culture, defined as 'superorganic', that sets humanity apart from the rest of the animal world, and that language is the hallmark of culture. But while culture is the defining attribute of the human species it is not part of some individual human nature, but is external to the individual: it is given only as part of the process of civilization, and 'civilization begins only where the individual ends.'[14] As a cultural determinist Kroeber was unwilling to allow any importance to the role of biology in the determination of human behaviour. We saw in the last chapter how Louis Malson put forward a culturalist argument of this type as an explanation of wolf children: their animal-like appearance and condition and lack of most normal human behaviour was the result, and not the cause, of their abandonment. Thus, isolation from human society, and the removal of a cultural environment, had 'de-humanized' such children. This is where the significance of cultural determinism for the ape language projects lies. If the lack of culture reduces a human being to a feral state, perhaps an attempt to 'humanize' an ape, to rear an infant chimpanzee within a human environment would provide the necessary stimulus to tap what was considered to be the ape's linguistic potential.

In 1931 Winthrop and Luella Kellogg acquired a seven month old chimpanzee and decided to bring it up in exactly the same manner as their ten-month-old-son. In their book *The Ape and the Child* they argued: 'Why not give one of the higher primates exactly the environmental advantages which a young child enjoys and then study the development of the resulting organism?'[15] So for nine months child and chimpanzee were treated identically, in order to record and measure their progress. At the end of that period, although the chimpanzee's comprehension of language was good (at fourteen months she understood over forty sentences) she had not managed to speak at all, and the Kelloggs considered the experiment a failure. But the project inspired another couple, Keith and Catherine Hayes, to repeat the experiment a decade and a half later. This project lasted seven years. Again the chimpanzee, a female named Viki, was treated as one of the family and was expected to join in the various familial activities. When the experiment ended, with Viki's death in 1954, the chimpanzee had learned four words, all spoken with a heavy accent, yet audible. Again, as with the Kelloggs' chimpanzee, Viki's comprehension of language far outstripped her production, and her obvious intelligence was demonstrated by her ability to score highly on a number of tests designed to discover her powers of understanding and classification. But, as with all the other apes, Viki's attempt to acquire spoken language was a failure. All the attempts to 'humanize' the ape, to provide a rich linguistic environment in the hope that this might facilitate language acquisition have met with little success. The question that had been asked in the eighteenth century reappeared: given their obvious intelligence and their ability to understand, and to act upon, spoken language commands, why do apes not speak? Is it because of physiological reasons or cognitive ones, in other words, do they lack the appropriate vocal apparatus to produce speech, or the appropriate neural structures necessary for language? In 1972 Philip Lieberman, a speech-sound analyst at the University of Connecticut, devised an experiment to test the former hypothesis, using computers to simulate the range of sounds produced by human and ape vocal chords. Desmond summarizes the results thus:

> Unlike man, who stands erect and whose larynx has descended down the neck to produce the extended 'organ pipe' region responsible for the full range of vocal sounds, the stooping ape is handicapped by truncated 'organ pipes'. Even though chimpanzees can generate sounds, they lack the optimum length of modulating air passage in the throat to articulate them into the critical vowels a, i, and u.[16]

This would tend to confirm the view that apes lack the vocal mechanisms necessary for speech, but, as Desmond points out, according to the computers chimpanzees should be able to produce a greater range of sounds than they actually do, 'a fact for which no one has yet produced an adequate explanation.'[17]

Although the Hayeses' attempts to teach Viki to speak were unsuccessful their experiment did provide the spur for another project, though in a completely unexpected way. The Hayeses had made a number of films of their sessions with Viki and it was while watching a video of one of them that Allen and Beatrice Gardner, psychologists at the University of Nevada at Reno, conceived the idea of using a manual sign language with a chimpanzee. They noticed, with the sound turned down, that Viki was perfectly capable of making herself understood through the use of gestures. If, as they suspected, Viki's inability to use language owed less to cognitive factors than it did to the mechanics of speech production, then the substitution of a manual, gestural language for a spoken one might still allow the possibility of a chimpanzee learning to use language. As behaviourists, the Gardners had more than a detached, scientific curiosity over the possible outcome, since they were involved in a fiercely combative intellectual dispute over the nature of language. The issue came to a head in 1957 with the publication of B.F. Skinner's *Verbal Behavior* and Noam Chomsky's very critical review of it in the journal *Language*. Skinner maintained that the essence of language is not to be found in any characteristic unique to the human species, but rather that language, as a form of verbal behaviour, is essentially no different from any other form of communication. As such, any animal, given the correct stimuli, conditioning, and reinforcement procedures, could be trained to use it.

The strength of feeling in Chomsky's review was a foretaste of the hostilities that were to ensue between the behaviourists and the linguists. 'Careful study' of Skinner's book, Chomsky wrote, demonstrates that his 'astonishing claims' about the nature of language 'are far from justified'. Moreover, it can be shown 'that the insights that have been achieved in the laboratories of the reinforcement theorist, though quite genuine, can be applied to complex human behaviour only in the most gross and superficial way.'[18] Chomsky argued that to explain language in terms of a stimulus-response model is mistaken because the capacity for language use is biologically pre-programmed in, and restricted to, human beings: 'If it were true in any deep sense that the basic processes in language are well understood and free of species restrictions, it would be extremely odd that language is limited to man.'[19]

For the Gardners the problem with the previous ape language projects was that, by focussing exclusively on spoken language, the experimenters were hindering the apes who were physiologically rather than mentally ill-equipped to produce vocal utterances. The use of a manual sign language would be more compatible with the stimulus-response model of learning, which is one of the cornerstones of behaviourist theory. The Gardners reasoned that through the use of a gestural language two-way communication between humans and a chimpanzee would demonstrate the linguistic abilities of the ape and strengthen the behaviourist argument. They decided to use American Sign Language (ASL), one of a number of gestural languages, because, being the primary language of the deaf population in North America and Canada (used by over half a million people), it had been recognized as a natural language, and its use by deaf children had been studied by linguists.

Each sign or gesture in ASL is made up of a number of basic units called cheremes, analogous to the phonemes used in spoken language. ASL has fifty-five cheremes, divided into three groups signifying hand configurations, the body location, and types of hand movement. Contrary to some critics' claims, only a minority of signs are iconic; the overwhelming majority are conventional, a fact that can be seen by examining the differences between ASL and other sign languages.

The Gardners began their project in the summer of 1966 with a one-year-old female chimpanzee called Washoe. By the time they published their first results in 1969, in a paper entitled 'Teaching sign language to a chimpanzee', Washoe had acquired over one hundred signs, and the Gardners were convinced that they had demonstrated the existence of linguistic-type abilities in a non-human primate. In 1971, when Washoe left the Gardners to take up residence at the Institute for Primate Studies in Oklahoma, she had learned to use 132 signs, and by 1975, 160, singly and in combinations.

The publication of the Gardners' first paper brought an immediate response from psychologists and linguists, and the first criticisms were not long in coming. To make matters worse, in proclaiming Washoe's linguistic successes the Gardners argued that they compared favourably with the language use of a two-and-a-half-year-old child. If the claim that a chimpanzee had acquired the use of a human sign language was controversial, then to compare its ability with that of a human child in the early stages of language development was guaranteed to raise the stakes even further.

Two important early criticisms of Washoe, in papers by Brown, and by Bronowski and Bellugi, concerned the question of whether the ape had a sense of grammar (whether she had a grasp of some of the more abstract qualities of language such as displacement and reconstitution), and her failure to ask questions. Roger Brown, in his paper 'The first sentences of child and chimp', addressed himself to the question of syntax. He argued that in using two sign combinations Washoe was just as likely to sign 'Washoe tickle' as she was 'tickle Washoe' when wanting to be tickled. That is, she did not demonstrate any knowledge of word order. Comparing Washoe's signing ability to the early language of young children, Brown argued that as children go on to master more complex grammatical forms it is possible to 'richly interpret' two-word combinations such as 'mommy lunch' as meaning 'mommy is eating her lunch'. Washoe on the other hand showed no signs of progressing to more complex sentence forms, and while it may be justifiable to compare her signings to the early utterances of young children, the Gardners' claim that Washoe's knowledge of language equalled that of a two-and-a-half-year-old was unjustified. For their part, the Gardners charged Brown with wanting to have his cake and eat it, claiming that when children reversed word order to him, it merely signalled the fact that they were on their way to a more complex understanding of language, but when Washoe did this it demonstrated her inability to grasp the complexities of language. The problem became even more complex when some linguists claimed that the issue was irrelevant as two-year-old children could not be said to use language. John Limber, in his paper 'Language in child and chimp' argued;

> Washoe, like most children during their second year, has achieved a considerable degree of proficiency in using arbitrary symbols to communicate. This is not to say, however, that Washoe, or most two year old children use a human language.[20]

As we can see, it is not simply a dispute between the behaviourism of the Gardners and the linguistics of Roger Brown. A number of linguists are themselves in disagreement, and not just over the question of whether two-year-old children have language but about the nature of language itself.

There exists no overall consensus as to a definition of language, and although Chomsky's work has been of considerable importance, it has not found unqualified acceptance among linguists. Thus, the question that concerns the Gardners and others, like Roger Fouts - does Washoe really have language? is becoming an intractable one. To make matters worse the 'ape-educators' are themselves deeply divided on these issues, a problem we shall return to below.

Bronowski and Bellugi, in their paper 'Language, name and concept', argue that the essence of human language lies in the twin qualities of displacement, the capacity to use language to refer to events and objects not concurrent with the immediate context, and reconstruction, the ability to reconstruct linguistic images and concepts in new combinations. They claim that Washoe's 'language' shows no evidence of either of these qualities. The absence of displacement and reconstitution, they argue, proves that these qualities are unique to the human mind.

The acid test of displacement and reconstitution, is of course, the generation of new signs or sentences; that is, using language in a new and creative way. Now, since the publication of the Gardners' early diaries of their work with Washoe, upon which Bronowski and Bellugi had based their claims, Washoe and a number of other chimpanzees trained in the use of ASL have been credited with the production both of new signs (termed 'creative naming') and new sentences. Washoe herself has coined the terms 'water bird' for a swan, and 'rock berry' for a Brazil nut; perhaps the most famous example is that of Lucy, another chimpanzee, who produced 'cry hurt food' after spitting out a radish. But these examples do not convince the sceptics who claim that the ape-educators have selected from a plethora of generally meaningless statements the small minority of combinations that succeed. Or so it might appear, as it is only these that are published. Until the complete transcripts of all the ape signings are published, including the mistakes, those that appear to be successful inventions can only stand as anecdotes.

The Gardners' experiments with Washoe were the first of a number of projects using chimpanzees trained in ASL, mostly conducted under the tutelage of Roger Fouts at the Institute for Primate Studies. While these experiments were taking place David Premack of the University of California was approaching the question of the apes' linguistic abilities from a different perspective. In 1966 Premack started a language analogue project with a six-year-old chimpanzee called Sarah. The Gardners had attempted to teach a human gestural language to Washoe in the hope of facilitating two way communication between human and ape. For this, the chimpanzee was immersed in the social and linguistic environment of a human family, to produce the most favourable conditions for the development of language; ASL was the language chosen in order to allow comparisons between Washoe and human children. Premack, on the other hand, was less interested in teaching a chimpanzee to communicate in a human language and more concerned with the logical processes underlying language use. He did not want to converse with Sarah, but to test her grasp of the cognitive structures upon which language is built. Consequently, much of Sarah's training involved solving problems of a linguistic nature. Rather than living as part of a human family Sarah was brought up in strict laboratory conditions, and the medium through which the experiments were conducted was not a human sign language but an artificial one invented by Premack. This consisted of a number of arbitrarily shaped and coloured signs, metal backed for use on a magnetic board. The signs represented words and names, like 'Sarah', 'Mary', 'apple', 'give', 'dish' etc., and each sign was arbitrary or conventional with respect to its referent, (for example, the sign for 'apple' was a blue plastic triangle). In order to receive rewards Sarah had to arrange the signs vertically on the magnetic board to form 'sentences', such as 'Mary give apple Sarah'. Initially the signs were used to evaluate Sarah's acquisition of fairly simple linguistic procedures, by enabling her to request certain foods, drinks, etc. and to comply with certain demands. As she became more adept at this Premack used the plastic sign 'language' to test Sarah's understanding of more abstract concepts, for example, by inventing a sign to represent 'name of', which would be inserted between the sign and its referent (between a blue plastic triangle and an apple, for instance), a procedure which allowed Sarah to grasp new nouns more quickly. Similarly, Premack invented signs representing 'colour of', 'size of', 'shape of' etc. to swell Sarah's vocabulary; 'same/different' to test her ability to discriminate between different sentences (is 'apple is red' 'same/different' as 'red colour of apple'?), and 'if/then' to assess her grasp of conditions. This last step was particularly revealing, for it demonstrated Sarah's ability to grasp the essential nature of a condition, to realize the consequences of following one course of action rather than another. For example, Sarah was presented with two different sentences, written vertically on to her magnetic board; they offered different choices, but with conditions: if Sarah take apple - then Mary give chocolate Sarah; if Sarah take banana - then Mary no give chocolate Sarah. Sarah was faced with the choice of having to forgo a piece of banana which she much preferred to a piece of apple, in order to obtain a piece of chocolate, which was far more desirable than either bananas or apples. As Desmond writes,

> To take that tortuous route to the coveted chocolate, Sarah had to scrutinise the sentence intently: she also had to grasp the essential nature of a condition - that if she took one step, another would surely follow. The upshot was that she had to think two jumps ahead.[21]

Even though Premack used a system involving plastic word signs instead of a manual sign language his work with Sarah still attracted the same criticisms as the Gardners' experiments with Washoe. Commenting on Sarah's success with Premack's tests the linguist Roger Brown wrote,

> Several things strike me as odd about Sarah's achievements; odd simply in the sense of not fitting easily into my framework of ideas. She seems to do about as well on one problem as another (generally correct about 70-80 per cent of

the time) in spite of what I, at least, think of as great differences of complexity among the problems.[22]

Brown is suggesting that Premack was unconsciously cueing his ape, unwittingly passing on non-verbal cues to the animal. This criticism has been levelled at a number of projects, particularly the Gardners' work with Washoe. In response, the Gardners adopted a 'double blind' method of experimentation, using two trainers; one asked the question of Washoe, and the other, without knowing what the question was, recorded her signs. Similarly, Premack developed a system whereby a trainer who had no knowledge of the meanings of the plastic signs was directed about which ones to write up on the board by a series of numbers written on the back of the signs. In both cases the apes' success rate fell from about 85 per cent to about 75 per cent. Neither of these systems satisfied the critics who still maintained that unconscious cueing was taking place.

These criticisms were strengthened by the work of Terrace, who from 1973 to 1977 was engaged on a sign language experiment with a chimpanzee called Nim. Terrace, a behavioural psychologist at Columbia University, began the project with the expectation of confirming the Gardners' findings and thus strengthening the behaviourists' anti-Chomskian arguments about language. During the project he was convinced that he had confirmed the Gardners' work. On studying over forty hours of videotapes of Nim's signing sessions, however, he was forced to change his mind. Only a small minority of Nim's signs were spontaneous, he claimed; the overwhelming majority were prompted unconsciously by his trainers. Similarly, the majority of the chimpanzee's signed responses contained signs that had only just been made by his trainers. In effect, Terrace argued, Nim was doing little more than repeating what had just been signed to him. Having begun the project convinced that Nim would provide evidence for the Gardners' behaviourist claims that an ape could learn to use a human language, Terrace concluded that on the contrary Nim demonstrated little evidence of what could be called language ability.[23]

If neither Premack's attempts at teaching a type of language ability to Sarah, nor the various sign language experiments did enough to satisfy the critics that there was no unconscious prompting on the part of the trainers, the only possible solution seemed to be the elimination of the human factor altogether. Duane Rumbaugh at the Georgia State University set up a language-analogue project with this aim in mind. Rumbaugh designed a set of experiments to test the linguistic abilities of a chimpanzee by inventing an artificial language which was activated via a computer. The language, entitled 'Yerkish' after Robert Yerkes, consisted of a number of lexigrams represented by keys mounted on to a computer console. The chimpanzee, named Lana, was taught to punch out the keys - whereby the lexigrams were illuminated on to a screen so that both Lana and her trainers could see the results - in a particular order to obtain whatever she wanted in the way of food or activity, or to show her compliance with certain demands. For example, to receive a banana, fruit juice, etc., or to watch her favourite film, she had to punch keys in the sequence to mean 'Please machine give. . . ' or 'Please machine show. . . .'

Though in appearance Rumbaugh's project was more similar to Premack's work than to the Gardners' - in keeping Lana in a laboratory rather than as a member of a human family, and using an artificially constructed language rather than a human one - his intention (to facilitate two way conversation between human and ape) was closer to the Gardners'. Rumbaugh was less interested in examining Lana's linguistic problem-solving abilities than in developing the attributes necessary for language production and encouraging Lana to initiate conversations. This point is particularly important, for one of the most persistent criticisms levelled at all the signing apes is that they rarely, if ever, initiate conversations but rather respond to questions and statements signed by their teachers. Two notable successes of the Lana project are that, first, the chimpanzee has been seen to initiate conversations, and second - and most unexpectedly - to ask questions of her teachers.[24]

Initially, the main area of disagreement in the ape language projects seemed to be between the behaviourists and the linguists over the nature of human language: the former arguing for their belief in a linguistic continuum across nature, and in the possibility of teaching language to other species, and the latter claiming language as a uniquely human attribute. However, as we saw earlier, the linguists themselves are divided as to the issues at hand, for while a number of experts were arguing over whether Washoe's signing abilities were comparable to those of two-year-old children in the early phases of language development, other linguists were claiming that the comparison was irrelevant as neither the ape nor two-year-old children could be said to be using language. Moreover, as the other ape language projects got under way it soon became clear that there existed no consensus among these either. Indeed, many of the most damning criticisms and counter criticisms were to come from within the ape camps themselves. The Gardners, for example, were quick to deny that the results achieved by either Premack or the Rumbaughs in any way merited comparison with those of Washoe, who was still, in their view, the only ape who had mastered the use of language. 'There is no reason to suppose', they argued, 'that Lana's productions have any semantic content.'[25] Similarly, Sarah, 'could have solved Premack's entire battery of problems by rote memory alone.'[26] The Gardners were just as dismissive of Premack's and Rumbaugh's methods as they were of Sarah's and Lana's achievements. Premack and Rumbaugh, they argued, 'despite the paraphernalia of the conventional laboratory such as caged subjects, elaborate hardware and elaborate software, and strict schedules of reinforcement . . . have fallen into some of the worst of the classical pitfalls.'[27] And again, 'the results that Premack and Rumbaugh *et al.* have presented thus far are more parsimoniously interpreted in terms of such classic factors as Clever Hans cues, rote memory, and learning sets.'[28]

For their part Rumbaugh and his associates echo the Gardners' criticism that Sarah could easily have learned all of Premack's tests by rote, without showing any indication that she had understood their communicative nature:

> Communication is a universal feature of language, but it was not initially the direct object of interest in the studies on Sarah. Her ability to communicate was clearly limited by the plastic chips available to her at any one time. Since she only worked on one problem at any given point, she did not have the option of communicating anything other than a correct or incorrect answer to that problem. This makes it difficult to understand how Sarah could come to realise that the plastic chips could be used to communicate desires and to control or orient the behaviour of others. It is also not clear that she viewed her trainers' use of these chips as a means of transmitting information or controlling her behaviour.[29]

Neither Sarah nor Washoe have convinced the Rumbaughs that their abilities are in any way similar to those necessary for the production and comprehension of language, and the Rumbaughs conclude, while there are abundant descriptions of very interesting and suggestive phenomena, there are few firm data, collected in controlled, blind test situations, to support the contention that either Washoe or Sarah are employing symbolically-mediated, abstract communication similar to that involved in human language.[30]

Clearly then, there exists no consensus among the various ape language projects as to the results achieved, but what of the initial objectives? Is there a measure of agreement as to what the main issues are? For the Gardners the issue is whether apes can use human language, a question which they answer with an emphatic 'yes'. Washoe had, they argued,

learned a natural human language and her early utterances were highly similar to, perhaps indistinguishable from, the early utterances of human children. Now, the categorical question, can a non-human being use a human language, must be replaced by quantitative questions; how much human language, how soon, or how far can they go?[31]

Nearly all the contributors to the ape language debates, be they psychologists, anthropologists, or linguists, agree with the Gardners that the issue is human language (though not of course with the Gardners' claims for their own ape). One notable exception is David Premack. Premack has been quoted as saying

Chimps do not have any significant degree of human language and when, in two to five years, this fact becomes properly disseminated, it will be of interest to ask, why we were so easily duped by the claim that they do.[32]

Premack, however, differs from the other experimenters; unlike the Gardners, who claim that Washoe has learned a human language, or Terrace, who started off with the same objective as the Gardners but who reached the opposite conclusion, his objective does not lie in assessing whether or not Sarah can be taught a human language. He wants to discover whether there exists in the mind of the ape the capacities necessary to deal with the conceptual, logical processes that underlie language, to see whether Sarah can grasp concepts such as 'same/different', and conditions such as 'if/then'.

The majority of those concerned directly with the ape language projects - the Gardners, Roger Fouts, the Rumbaughs, etc. - and sympathizers like Eugene Linden, are convinced that some apes have acquired, albeit in a limited capacity, the use of a human language; whereas the majority of linguists and anthropologists are equally convinced to the contrary. But the problem of confronting the debate head on, so to speak, is that the question that lies at the heart of the issue, 'can apes really use human language?' is one that makes little sense to ask. As Philip Lieberman has pointed out, 'Asking whether chimpanzees have language is pointless and silly when you've already restricted the scope of the word 'language' to linguistic ability equivalent to that of present day homo sapiens.'[33]

But it is not only a question of definition, although it is true that there exists a plethora of definitions of language, some of which would allow for the possibility of linguistic apes, and others of which restrict the facility to human speech. Indeed, as we saw earlier when discussing the child/chimpanzee comparisons drawn by the Gardners, a number of linguists argued that the question of comparison was largely irrelevant as in neither case was language being used. More than this, it is necessary to realise that what one is confronted with is less a dispute over facts than a question of assumptions: the dispute is not so much a resolvable issue as an ideological stalemate. The ape language experiments exhibit a marked degree of anthropocentrism; this, moreover, is more in evidence - paradoxically - among the 'ape educators' themselves than among the linguists and anthropologists who argue for human uniqueness and heatedly deny the apes' linguistic abilities. The question 'Can apes really use human language?' is built upon an outdated metaphysics because it uses humanity as the yardstick for measuring the apes' 'progress'. By placing humanity at the apex of creation it owes more to the great chain of being than to evolutionary theory. The question that the debates set out to answer is both an impossible and an irrelevant one. Unfortunately, by using it to establish a frame of reference for the debates, the genuinely important aspects of the experiments are sadly neglected. By focusing so strongly on the question of human language and on the need to defend a qualitative distinction between human and animal, it overlooks the apes' ability to manipulate arbitrary symbols creatively, one of the necessary processes upon which language is built, and an ability readily recognized by all parties in the dispute, even the strongest critics of the experiments.

The fact that the species closest to humanity has been shown to possess many of the capacities necessary for the development of linguistic skills (a grasp of concepts, the ability to recognise the relationship between a sign and its referent, the ability to string signs together, and to construct new ones; the ability to ask questions) has been obscured by the argument about the uniqueness of human language. The remarkable achievements of the ape in being able to learn to use linguistic signs when it has no natural language - a facility which, in human beings after all has only evolved slowly over thousands, perhaps millions, of years - are used instead to provide theoretical support for an intellectually sterile position on the nature of language and human behaviour. It is one thing to maintain an argument against human uniqueness, to confront the 'only humans can . . .' type of argument - indeed, this has been one of the objectives of this book. But it is quite another thing to do so in defence of a theory which postulates the crudest type of explanation of human and animal behaviour. Commenting on B.F. Skinner's own admission of surprise that his work had remained free of species restrictions Desmond notes, 'The ability to achieve the same results regardless of the astonishing diversity of his subject species strikes me as a slamming indictment: a measure of his failure, not his success.'[34]

The position of the 'ape educators' becomes even more problematic when it is realized that the argument over language can only be won at the expense of robbing the ape of its species sovereignty: success in the field of language results in the ape being able to ascend a few rungs of the ladder in the direction of humanity. What price a cultured ape?

6
Conclusion

I have been concerned to examine the oppositions between nature and culture and human and animal, and their role in social theory. One of my main arguments has been that the human sciences have inherited from the Enlightenment a conception of the human as unique, and of culture as qualitatively different from, and superior to, nature; and that these distinctions have continued to command an important place in social theories. In an attempt to preserve their exclusive grip on the study of 'man' the human sciences - by pressing claims for the autonomy of culture and the uniqueness of the human - have maintained these hierarchical relationships between 'man' and nature, nature and culture. Indeed, their retention has led to the development of an equally rigid distinction between instinct and learning. As I argued when discussing the debates on feral children and apes and language, the thesis that humans, unlike animals, exhibit no instincts that underlie behaviour, that human nature is 'infinitely malleable', is one which underpins many culturalist/behaviourist accounts. Moreover, as I insisted in chapter 1, cultural anthropology was itself founded upon an explicit rejection of instinct theory: learning replaces instinct in the human species; human behaviour is the product of culture and, as such, can only be understood in the terms of culture. One consequence of this position is that, in recoiling so strongly from an approach which seeks to reduce human behaviour to a bundle of biologically determined instincts, many human scientists have turned instead to an equally crude and deterministic mirror opposite. To say that in humans learning does replace instinct, that human behaviour is entirely a product of social relations is to declare 'man' a *tabula rasa*. Could any creature as complex as a human being be as totally malleable as the *tabula rasa* metaphor suggests? As Mary Midgley

102

has written we are, after all, animals, not gods or fairies.[1] Rigid oppositions between nature and culture, human and animal are dangerous - they obscure more than they reveal. As Peter Reynolds has argued, the opposition between nature and culture 'does not rest on validated differences between humans and other animals but on a hierarchical concept of the relationship between man and nature that owes nothing to the study of primates whatsoever.'[2] If the theory of evolution is to be accepted, he argues, then

> the behavioural differences among primates must be explicable as the product of transformation over time. However, the anthropological strategy . . . has been to regard these transformations as leading to a level of organization in man that can be explained without recourse to these so-called lower levels: an evolutionary emergent of collective representations, social facts, conventions and institutions. The existence of such phenomena is not in question, but the methodological claim that such phenomena constitute a level of organization that can be understood without reference to psychobiological variables is a very strong claim indeed, and it is not easily reconciled with the findings of natural science.[3]

So, to declare, as do many anthropologists, that culture is a separate level of distinctly human organization in no way vitiates the need to understand what the behavioural differences between humans and other primates are, or what types of evolutionary transformation our prehuman ancestors had to undergo in order to evolve into *Homo sapiens*.[4]

Rather than claiming then, that human behaviour is the product of different principles from that of other animals, 'it would be more correct to say that it is constituted on *additional* principles, but these additions can by no means be assumed to invalidate all that has gone before or to exist in a biological vacuum.'[5]

Oppositions between nature and culture, human and animal display not only our ignorance of other animal species, but also of ourselves. Certainly some species demonstrate the existence of genetically determined instinctive behaviour, or what should more properly be called 'closed instincts', that is, fixed patterns of behaviour exactly reproduced even in creatures reared in isolation, such as the bees' honey dance, and some types of bird song. But the distinction between instinct and learning, in so far as it is controlled by the distinction between nature and culture, is not relevant for primates; much primate behaviour, human included, develops through both innate and environmental factors and both are necessary for mature development. Non-human primates raised in isolation develop severely abnormal forms of behaviour quite unlike that of their natural environment. Even language, traditionally seen as the cultural phenomenon *par excellence* develops through the interaction of both social and biological elements. As the discussion of Genie in chapter four demonstrated, Eric Lenneberg's work suggests that a critical period exists for the normal development of language, after which its acquisition becomes increasingly difficult. Interestingly, the 'critical period' theory developed from research on songbirds. Whereas the call repertoire of most birds is purely instinctual, in songbirds instinct and learning combine to produce a more complex phenomenon. In some species song learning is confined to a critical period when the bird is between ten and fifty days of age; beyond then the learning of a normal song is impossible. Moreover, in some species a specific model is required. A male white-crowned sparrow, if exposed to an adult white-crowned song during the critical period, will develop a normal adult song. If exposed to the song of a different species, however, the bird will develop an abnormal song of the white-crowned type. In some cases the bird will develop the entire song of a foster parent of another species. For example, a male zebra finch imitated the song of a male Bengalese finch. This could happen even if the bird later heard the song of the male of its own species. Reynolds writes

> although birds are phylogenetically remote from primates, they are the only other group of vertebrates, with the possible exception of whales and dolphins, known to have developed traditionally transmitted vocal communication. Like in man too, their vocal productions are controlled by one side of the brain. As such, vocal learning in birds cannot be dismissed as too remote from man to permit comparison.[6]

Similarly, the linguist Noam Chomsky argues that although the particular language that children learn varies according to their cultural environment, the fact that they *can* learn a language may well be a product of complex bio-programming in the human brain.[7]

These arguments should suggest caution when making pronouncements as to the autonomy of human culture, and a rigid distinction between instinct and learning, human and animal. To recognize our common evolutionary ancestry with other primates does not necessitate taking on board the 'naked ape' type arguments of Desmond Morris, or the wilder claims of sociobiology. If evolutionary theory is correct, then there are no truly essential differences between humans and other animals. To speak of human uniqueness is quite acceptable, as long as we are prepared to accept that chimpanzees, dolphins, bees, and humming-birds are also unique. But, as we have seen, when discussing Levi-Strauss, Sahlins *et al.*, one of the problems with maintaining a rigid distinction between nature and culture, or human and animal, is that it leads to just such claims for the autonomy of culture, or for human uniqueness; a hundred years after the death of Darwin many human scientists act as if humans really were the product of a separate creation. And it is not just in anthropology that these arguments are heard. Consider the following

> learned behaviour - ideas, techniques and habits passed on by one generation to another - in a sense a social heritage. . . . This learned behaviour, or social inheritance, of any society is called its culture. It is the possession of a common culture, and the ability to communicate and pass it on to others that distinguishes the human being from other animals. Humans are human because they possess culture.[8]

This is taken from an introductory sociology text currently in use in universities throughout the country. The problem with such texts, is that arguments claiming human uniqueness or the autonomy of culture always begin to break down when the capacities selected as the criteria to establish that uniqueness or autonomy can be shown to exist - in however crude or rudimentary a form - in other species. This desire to draw a circle around the human, to maintain arguments that begin 'only humans can. . . ' or 'only humans have . . .' relies upon an ontological essentialism. As Adrian Desmond has remarked, 'absence of evidence is not evidence of absence';[9] as soon as evidence does appear in other species, the argument begins to fall down.

The point I am making here is not to diminish the claims made for culture by advancing the pertinence of biology. What I am contesting is the philosophical habit of pitting one against the other. The problem is a conceptual and complex one and one which raises the question of the relation between the human sciences and metaphysical dogma. What is objectionable about categories of human uniqueness and the autonomy of culture is that they serve to foreclose the analysis of human attributes. By always already knowing the world in terms of the distinction between nature and culture we are prevented from setting up new problems in new ways, and we are condemned to repeat static formulas as if they were sacred truths.

Traditionally, the favourite candidates for demonstrating human uniqueness have been language, tool-use and tool-making, self-awareness, and learned behaviour or culture. As we saw in chapter 5, chimpanzees trained in the use of ASL have demonstrated a wide ability to manipulate linguistic symbols in a meaningful and creative way, and to construct new signs. In addition, the projects led by David Premack and Duane Rumbaugh have shown that chimpanzees like Sarah and Lana have achieved much success in experiments designed to test their knowledge of the logical and abstract processes upon which language is built. The question as to whether chimpanzees really have language is not, or should not be, the main issue, and nor are comparisons with two-year-old children.[10] We should not be trying to 'prove' that chimpanzees have or do not have human language, but rather to understand what the ape's undoubted ability can tell us about the nature of language and what further insights it can give us about the mind of the ape. The fact that chimps do possess these abilities, however, means that the claim that language represents a fundamental discontinuity between the human mind and the mind of the ape is by no means unproblematic.

Like language the ability to use tools has long been regarded as an ability unique to the human species. But again, recent research casts doubt on such a claim. The observations of wild chimpanzees by Jane Goodall, carried out over more than twenty years in the Gombe National Park in Tanzania, have furnished ample evidence to the contrary. Goodall's graphic descriptions of Mike - a formerly low ranking male, using empty kerosene cans to enhance his charging displays and thus terrorize his rivals into submission, is a vivid example of the ape's intelligent use of an external object for a specific purpose.[11] But perhaps more remarkable have been the examples of chimpanzees selecting and modifying twigs for use as probes in their collective and regular bouts of termite 'fishing'. A number of commentators have testified to the complexities involved in the activity of termite fishing; one, Geza Teleki, spent some months laboriously trying to match the apes' skills, but with little success: Teleki considered his efforts to be on a par with those of a four-year-old chimp. Such behaviour demonstrates how important learning is in chimpanzee social life. The skills involved in termite fishing are only acquired slowly, though all the animals in the group learn them; the neighbouring baboons, on the contrary, seemed unable to develop the necessary technique. This is how Teleki sums up his experience:

> Incompetent as they were, my attempts to acquire the skills of locating tunnels, selecting materials, inserting probes and extracting termites left me with a healthy measure of respect for chimpanzee technical ability, as well as with a nagging suspicion that the physical and psychological capabilities needed to develop, apply and transmit such skills may differ in degree but not in kind from those needed by humans (hunter-gatherers) to locate, expose and gather insects and subsurface flora.[12]

As with tool-use, so with self-awareness: the ability to recognize one's self-image has long been assumed to be a uniquely human one. Indeed, sociological theory has often insisted on an inseparable link between self-awareness and language. For G.H. Mead language was a necessary condition for the development of self-awareness. Children, in what Mead called the game stage, develop an awareness of self by role-playing; taking on the roles of 'significant others', talking back to themselves, and internalizing their dialogues with themselves. Mead, of course, thought that self-awareness was confined to humans. But in the mid-1970s American psychologist Gordon Gallup devised a series of experiments designed to test self-awareness in non-human primates. Gallup reasoned that, as with human children, any potential that chimpanzees might have for self-awareness would only develop gradually; thus the experiments, initially using chimpanzees and orang-utans, involved long-term exposure to full length mirrors. The animals' behaviour and reactions were recorded and divided into socially directed (reacting as if to an intruder, bobbing, threatening, etc.) and self-directed behaviour. After a few days the self-directed behaviour increased dramatically. As Gallup writes,

Such self-directed responding took the form of grooming parts of the body which would otherwise be visually inaccessible without the mirror, picking bits of food from between the teeth while watching the mirror image... picking extraneous material from the nose by inspecting the reflected image.... In all instances of self-directed behaviour, the self is the referent through the reflection, whereas in cases of social behaviour the reflection is the referent.[13]

Further evidence for self-awareness was furnished when Gallup anaesthetized the apes and painted an odourless red dye on to their foreheads. When the animals came round and were re-exposed to the mirror they immediately examined their foreheads (in the mirror) rubbing the red patches and smelling their fingers. As Gallup argues,

if the reflection was still being interpreted as *another* animal there could be no reason for the chimps to smell or look at their own fingers ... because these would not have been the fingers that made actual contact with the red spots.[14]

Finally, numerous examples of learned behaviour among non-human primates have been documented. Perhaps the best recorded concerns the macaque monkeys on the Japanese island of Koshima.[15] When scientists first began studying the animals in the early 1950s they left sweet potatoes in the sand in order to observe the macaques. One female, known to the researchers as Imo, began washing the dirt and sand from the potatoes before eating them, a practice which, over the course of a few months, gradually spread to other members of the group until it had become a habit. Sometime later, the scientists began throwing rice into the sand in an attempt to observe the macaques in greater detail. The same female, Imo, picked up handfuls of the rice and sand, threw them into the sea, whereupon the sand sank and enabled her to scoop up the rice, thus avoiding the laborious task of separating each grain of rice from the sand. Again, over the course of a few months Imo's innovative behaviour spread to the rest of the group, with the exception of the eldest members, and became an everyday occurrence. Both of these examples demonstrate the existence of learned and shared behaviour among a group of non-human primates, features which human scientists have traditionally linked with the possession of culture. Now, neither of these examples, nor the others previously discussed are meant in any way to diminish the very large differences that clearly do exist between humans and other primate species. What they do indicate, however, is that these differences are the products of evolutionary transformation and not of a - theoretically - unbridgeable gap between ourselves and other species. Each of these examples, although perhaps in themselves trivial, demonstrates that arguments for human uniqueness and the autonomy of culture become increasingly difficult to maintain as our knowledge of other animal species increases. Human capacities and abilities are the product of evolution, they are not gifts from God.

The argument for the rejection of the nature/culture opposition is not germane just to the question of the relationship between humans and other animals. It can be shown that in areas that are central to sociology, like sexuality, the opposition is a persistent obstacle. In a justified attempt to criticize sociobiological approaches, where sexuality is seen as natural, unchanging, the product of a biologically determined instinct,[16] sociologists have often responded with the claim that it is 'socially constructed', a complex set of learned behaviours. This position is merely the other side of the determinist coin, a form of sociological essentialism. Even in attempts to criticize the nature/culture opposition recourse is often made to just such an opposition:

> Women and men are products of social relations, if we change the social relations, we change the categories 'woman' and 'man'. . . we would argue that, to put it at its bluntest, social relations determine sex differences rather than biological sex producing social divisions between the sexes.[17]

But to say that women and men are the product of social relations is to return us again to the difficulties inherent in the *tabula rasa* myth. For paradoxically it is this myth which exercises the most tyrannical grip on the human sciences. It might seem as though the doctrine of the *tabula rasa*, of all differences being socially constructed was a productive way out of being governed by all the petty essentialisms of common sense where everyday folklore insists that humans are naturally like this, or like that. Indeed perhaps such a view once had a polemical virtue. But now it has turned into its own dogma: that whatever is constructed is ultimately socially constructed and indeed that what has been constructed can be infinitely reconstructed. This is the metaphysical essentialism of much social science. My argument has been not to bend the stick the other way, as to demonstrate that the division of the world into enclosed worlds of nature and culture is itself the obstacle to the analysis of humans as constructions. To recognize that sexuality is organized through, and is dependent upon a complex set of social forms does not justify the claims for social construction that are often made. The leap from social organization to social construction is unwarranted. As the discussion of Freud's work in chapter 2 argued, if the theory of psychoanalysis has any validity, then sexuality is the complex product of a number of factors - social, biological, and psychic; it cannot be made to reside either in the realm simply of biology or of culture. The revolutionary concept of the unconscious, viewed from a logical point of view, has perhaps been so productive precisely because it is thought outside the opposition of nature and culture.

As a means both for demarcating a specific field of phenomena - an autonomous realm of social and cultural facts - and for providing forms of explanation of those phenomena, an ontological division between nature and culture is thus tautological: a conceptual distinction is invoked as the means by which it itself is explained. The human sciences do not need to resort to the metaphysical dualism and attendant forms of essentialism that such oppositions entail. The problem with the notion of the autonomy of culture is not that it acts as a rallying call for the human sciences, defending them from being subsumed under one grand sociobiological scheme. The human sciences possess effective and necessary methods of study, concepts and theories, which prevent them from losing their independence. The problem with the way in which the autonomy of culture has been used in the human sciences concerns the claim that social and cultural phenomena, human behaviour etc., can only be understood in terms of culture. Culture becomes a self enclosed and unified entity which governs and directs the behaviour of individuals in an all-embracing and exclusive way. It is possible, and indeed sometimes necessary, to challenge the pertinence of biological explanations of human behaviour with respect to substantive issues, but not to deny them any validity in principle. But this is often what has characterized the extreme reactions of sociologists to sociobiology.[18] Sociologists have opposed sociobiology on its first premise, but in so doing have substituted one equally as dogmatic. Thus culture rather than biology is exclusively privileged. The human sciences here do themselves a disservice; not simply by descending to the arguments of reductionism, but in so doing by employing the machinery of metaphysics as the means by which those arguments are conducted. For a point by point substitution of culture for biology not only tends to avoid confronting issues of biology: it also elevates culture into a totalizing explanation for human behaviour and institutions. To use the concept of culture as a pre-given and exhaustive totality is in fact to replace one form of metaphysics with another. The analysis of social relations could only profit from giving the slip to metaphysics of whatever hue.

Notes

Introduction.

1. Plato (1970) p. 137.
2. Ibid. p. 130.
3. Ibid. pp. 187–8.
4. Hobbes. (1981) p. 186.
5. Ibid. p. 223.
6. Locke (1966) p. 6
7. Rousseau (1973) p. 38.
8. Throughout this text the 'human' sciences will be used in preference to 'social' sciences. This is because in Great Britain 'social' science is usually used to refer to the disciplines of sociology and economics, whereas in France, the term 'human sciences' includes anthropology and psychoanalysis also. As I shall be concerned with the latter two disciplines as well as with sociology, I have chosen to adopt this usage.
9. White (1949) p. 15.
10. For Homer on 'savages', see Ferguson (1975), ch. 1; see also Sandars (1972).

Chapter 1

1. Stocking (1982) p. 47.
2. Ibid. p. 119.
3. Reynolds (1981) p. 4.
4. Ibid. p. 9.
5. Quoted in Stocking (1982) p. 113.
6. Quoted in Desmond (1979) p. 162.
7. Jones (1980) pp. 141-42.
8. Ibid. p. 142.
9. Hofstadter (1955) p. 161.
10. Galton, quoted in Jones (1980) p. 99
11. Freeman (1983) p. 8.
12. Ibid. pp. 8-9.
13. Ibid. p. 15.
14. See Freeman (1983) p. 37.
15. Tylor (1913) p. 2.
16. Ibid. p. 1.
17. Stocking (1982) p. 73.
18. Ibid. p. 74.
19. Quoted in Stocking (1982) p. 81.
20. Stocking (1982) p. 203.
21. Ibid. p. 152.
22. Galton, quoted in Freeman (1983) p. 10.

23. Quoted in Freeman (1983) p. 5.
24. Boas (1938) p. 195.
25. Stocking (1982) p. 264.
26. Cravens (1978) p. 91–2
27. Freeman (1983) pp. 45-6.
28. Stocking (1982) p. 306.
29. Kroeber (1952), p. 22.
30. Kroeber, quoted in Freeman (1983) p. 40.
31. Kroeber (1952) pp. 24-5.
32. Ibid. p. 26.
33. Ibid. p. 27.
34. Ibid. p. 22.
35. Ibid. p. 27.
36. Ibid. p. 27.
37. Ibid. p. 28.
38. Ibid. p. 31.
39. Ibid. p. 32.
40. Ibid. p. 32.
41. Ibid. p. 32.
42. Ibid. p. 20.
43. Stocking (1982) p. 259.
44. Freeman (1983) p. 42.
45. Kroeber (1952) p. 38.
46. Ibid. p. 38
47. Ibid. p. 40.
48. Ibid. p. 41.
49. Ibid. p. 41.
50. Ibid. p. 49.
51. Ibid. p. 49.
52. Quoted in Kroeber (1952) p. 40.
53. Ibid. p. 40.
54. Carneiro (1981) p. 210.
55. White, quoted in Carneiro (1981) p. 214.
56. White (1949) p. 364.
57. Ibid. p. 364.
58. Ibid. p. 365.
59. Ibid. p. 366.
60. Ibid. p. 366.
61. Ibid. p. 368.
62. Ibid. pp. 368-9.
63. Ibid. p. 22.
64. Ibid. p. 25.
65. Ibid. p. 33.
66. Ibid. p. 45.
67. White, quoted in Carneiro (1981) p. 236.
68. Sahlins (1976) p. 101.
69. Ibid. p. 102.
70. Ibid. p. viii.
71. Ibid. p. 58.
72. Ibid. p. 58.

73. Ibid. pp. 60-1.
74. Ibid. p. 62.
75. Ibid. p. 73.
76. Ibid. p. 74.
77. Ibid. p. 76.
78. Ibid. p. 83.
79. Ibid. p. 102.
80. Ibid. p. 206.
81. Ibid. p. 169.
82. Ibid. p. 181.
83. Ibid. p. 181.
84. Ibid. p. 176.

Chapter 2

1. Derrida (1970) p. 250.
2. Levi-Strauss (1966) p. 13.
3. Ibid. p. 15.
4. Ibid. p. 17.
5. Ibid. p. 35.
6. Ibid. p. 9.
7. Ibid. p. 75.
8. Ibid. p. 217.
9. Ibid. p. 75.
10. Ibid. p. 80.
11. Ibid. p. 115.
12. Levi-Strauss (1964) p. 77.
13. Ibid. p. 89.
14. Levi-Strauss (1966), p. 135.
15. Ibid. pp. 75-6.
16. Ibid. p. 135.
17. Levi-Strauss (1964) p. 90.
18. See Jenkins (1979) pp. 17-18.
19. Jacobson, quoted in Jenkins (1979) p. 18.
20. Levi-Strauss (1963) pp. 58.
21. Ibid. pp. 58-9.
22. Ibid. p. 34.
23. Goody (1977) p. 64.
24. MacCormack (1980) p. 10.
25. Strathern (1980) p. 179.
26. Levi-Strauss (1969) p. 3.
27. Ibid. p. 4.
28. Ibid. p. 5.
29. Ibid. p. 8.
30. Ibid. pp. 8-9.
31. Ibid. p. 10.
32. Ibid. p. 9.
33. Ibid. pp. 24-5.

34. Ibid. p. 479.
35. Ibid. p. 481.
36. Ibid. p. 32.
37. Ibid. p. 37.
38. Laplanche and Pontalis (1973) p. 214.
39. Freud, quoted in above, p. 215.
40. Hirst and Woolley (1982) p. 144.
41. Freud, quoted in Laplanche and Pontalis (1973) p. 30.
42. Freud (1977) p. 98.
43. Hirst and Woolley (1982) p. 146.
44. Freud (1977) p. 57.
45. Ford and Beach (1952) p. 207.
46. Beach (1947) p. 310. See also Nadler and Braggio (1974)p.548: The importance of early social interaction for behavioural development in primates has been demonstrated most convincingly in studies of animals deprived of such early experience. Rhesus monkeys and chimpanzees reared in social isolation not only failed to develop appropriate sexual orientation, but demonstrated little efficiency, if any, in general social behaviour. Also Suomi *et al.* (1974) p. 528.
47. Levi-Strauss, quoted in Jenkins (1979) p. 9.
48. Levi-Strauss (1963) p. 356.
49. Ibid. p. 358.

Chapter 3

1. Boas and Lovejoy (1935) p. 7.
2. Ibid. p. 8.
3. Ibid. p. 288.
4. Tacitus (1970) p. 130.
5. Volckler, quoted in Ferguson (1975) p. 12.
6. Tacitus (1970) p. 102.
7. Ibid. p. 104.
8. Ibid. p. 118.
9. Ibid. p. 121.
10. Quoted in Boas (1948) p. 137.
11. Ibid. p. 135.
12. Ibid. p. 134.
13. Wittkower (1975).
14. Quoted in Boas (1948) p.
15. Wittkower (1975) p. 72.
16. Foucault (1970) p. 129.
17. Lovejoy (1964) p. 52.
18. Ibid. p. 58.
19. Ibid. p. 59.
20. Ibid. p. 60.
21. Hodgen (1964) p. 408.
22. Ibid. p. 409.
23. Burke (1972) p. 263.

24. Bernheimer (1952) p. 112.
25. Dudley and Novack (1972) p. x.
26. Bernheimer (1952) pp. 43-4.
27. White (1972) p. 22.
28. Bernheimer (1952) p. 18.
29. Ibid. p. 19.

Chapter 4

1. Atkinson (1920) p. ix.
2. Ibid. p. 3.
3. Ibid. p. x.
4. Symcox (1972) p. 227.
5. Ibid. p. 227.
6. Smith (1960) p. 6.
7. Ibid. p. 7.
8. Ibid. p. 110.
9. Ibid. p. 5.
10. Lovejoy (1948) pp. 22, 24.
11. Symcox (1972) p. 230.
12. Hirst and Woolley (1985) p. 152.
13. Wokler (1976) p. 2302.
14. Janson (1952) p. 336.
15. Lovejoy (1964) p. 234.
16. Wokler (1976) p. 2305.
17. Monboddo, quoted in Lovejoy (1948) p. 47.
18. Ibid. p. 48.
19. See Aarsleff (1983a) p. 285.
20. Rousseau (1973) p. 284.
21. Quoted in Symcox (1972) p. 232.
22. Descartes, quoted in Lane (1979) p. 23.
23. Quoted in Aarsleff (1967) pp.38-9.
24. Aarsleff (1982) p. 278.
25. See Novack (1972).
26. Pinel, quoted in Lane (1979) p. 56.
27. Itard, in Malson (1972) p. 96.
28. Ibid. p. 99.
29. Stam (1976) pp. 46-7.
30. Condillac (1974) p. 102.
31. Itard in Malson (1972) p. 142.
32. Ibid. p. 179.
33. See Zingg (1940).
34. Curtiss (1977) p. 9.
35. Bettelheim (1967) p. 347.
36. Ibid. p. 347.

Chapter 5

1. Patterson (1978) p. 95.
2. Seidenberg and Petitto, quoted in Desmond (1979) p. 53.
3. Descartes (1968) pp. 74-5
4. Lieberman (1976) p. 14.
5. Hymes (1974) p. 10.
6. Chomsky (1980) p. 239.
7. Chomsky (1972) pp. 66-7.
8. Reynolds (1980) pp. 45-6.
9. La Mettrie, quoted in Fouts and Rigby (1980) p. 262.
10. Yorkes, quoted in above, p. 262.
11. Quoted in Desmond (1979) p. 62.
12. Ibid. p. 62.
13. Desmond (1979) p. 68.
14. Kroeber, quoted in Desmond (1979) p. 74.
15. Quoted in Desmond (1979) p. 80.
16. Desmond (1979) p. 29.
17. Ibid. p. 29.
18. Chomsky (1959) p. 28
19. Ibid. p. 30n.
20. Limber (1980) p. 205.
21. Desmond (1979) p. 122.
22. Quoted in Desmond (1979) p. 96.
23. See Terrace (1980).
24. See Desmond (1979) pp. 100-1.
25. Gardner and Gardner (1980) p. 317.
26. Ibid. p. 316.
27. Ibid. p. 313.
28. Ibid. pp. 317-18.
29. Savage-Rumbaugh and Rumbaugh (1980) p. 353-83
30. Ibid. p. 381.
31. Gardner and Gardner (1980) p. 329.
32. Premack, quoted in Desmond (1979) p. 152.
33. Lieberman (1976) p. 14.
34. Desmond (1979) p. 85.

Conclusion

1. Midgley (1980a) p. 55.
2. Reynolds (1981) p. 69.
3. Ibid. p. 70.
4. Ibid. p. 72.
5. Ibid. p. 72.
6. Ibid. p. 23.
7. See Chomsky (1972)
8 Bilton *et al* (1981) p. 10
9. Desmond (1979) p. 176

10. Two of the criticisms levelled at the ape-language experiments are that the animals do not ask questions, and do not initiate conversations, but only respond to promptings from their trainers. Interestingly, both of these points are mentioned by Susan Curtiss with respect to Genie. Indeed, Curtiss compares Genie's acquisition of language to that of the chimpanzees in the ape-language experiments. See Curtiss (1977) pp. 210-11 and 233-4.
11. See Goodall (1974) pp. 117-20. See also p. 105.
12. Quoted in Desmond (1979) p. 146. See also Goodall (1974) pp. 47-9.
13. Quoted in Desmond (1979) pp. 173-4.
14. Ibid p. 174.
15. See Attenborough (1979) pp. 281-2
16. See Symons (1979) esp. p. v.
17. Brown and Jordanova (1981) p. 231.
18. See Allen *et al* (1978).

Bibliography

Aarsleff, H. (1967) *The Study of Language in England 1780-1860*, Princeton, NJ: Princeton University Press.

—— (1976) 'An outline of language-origins theory since the renaissance', *Annals of the New York Academy of Sciences* 280.

—— (1982) *From Locke to Saussure: Essays on the Study of Language and Intellectual History*, London: Athlone Press.

Aitchison, J. (1976) *The Articulate Mammal*, London: Hutchinson.

Alexander, M. (1977) *Omai: Noble Savage*, London: Collins.

Allen, E. *et al.* (1978) 'Against Sociobiology', quoted in Caplan (ed.) *The Sociobiology Debate*, New York: Harper & Row.

Ashcraft, R. (1972) 'Leviathan triumphant: Thomas Hobbes and the politics of wild man', in E. Dudley and M. Novack (eds) *The Wild Man within*, Pittsburgh, Pa.: University of Pittsburgh Press.

Atkinson, G. (1920) *The 'Extraordinary Voyage' in French Literature Before 1700*, New York: Columbia University Press.

—— (1922) *The 'Extraordinary Voyage' in French Literature from 1700-1720*, Paris: Librairie Ancienne Honore Champion.

Attenborough, R. (1979) *Life on Earth*, London: Collins.

Beach, F. (1947) 'Evolutionary Changes in the Physiological Control of Mating Behaviour in Mammals', *The Psychological Review* 54, 6.

Benoist, J-M (1978) *The Structural Revolution*, London: Weidenfeld & Nicolson.

Benton, T. (1984) 'Biological ideas and their cultural uses', in S.C. Brown (ed.) *Objectivity and Cultural Divergence*, Cambridge: Cambridge University Press.

Bernheimer, R. (1952) *Wild Men in the Middle Ages: a Study in Art, Sentiment, and Demonology*, Cambridge, Mass: Harvard University Press.

Bettelheim, B. (1959) 'Feral children and autistic children'; *American Journal of Sociology*.

—— (1967) *The Empty Fortress*, New York: The Free Press.

Bilton, A. (1981) *Introductory Sociology*, London: Macmillan.

Boas, F. (1938) *The Mind of Primitive Man*, New York: Macmillan.

Boas, G. (1948) Essays on *Primitivism and Related Ideas in the Middle Ages*, Baltimore: The Johns Hopkins University Press.

—— and Lovejoy, A.O. (1935) *Primitivism and Related Ideas in Antiquity*, Baltimore: The Johns Hopkins University Press.

Bronowski, J. and Bellugi, B. (1980) 'Language, name, and concept', in T.A. Sebeok and J.V. Sebeok (eds) *Speaking of Apes: a Critical Anthology of Two-way Communications with Man*, New York: Plenum.

Brown, P. and Jordanova, L. (1981) 'Oppressive dichotomies: the nature/culture debate', in Cambridge Women's Studies Group, London: Virago.

Brown, R. (1958) *Words and Things*, New York: The Free Press.

—— (1980) 'The First Sentences of Child and Chimp' in T.A. Sebeok and J.V. Sebeok (eds) *Speaking of Apes: a Critical Anthology of Two-way Communication with Man*, New York: Plenum.

Brown, S.C. (ed) (1984) *Objectivity and Cultural Divergence*, Cambridge: Cambridge University Press.

Burke, J.G. (1972) 'The wild man's pedigree: scientific method and racial anthropology', in E. Dudley and M. Novack (eds) *The Wild Man Within*, Pittsburgh Pa.: University of Pittsburgh Press.

Burrow, J.W. (1966) *Evolution and Society*, Cambridge: Cambridge University Press.

Cambridge Women's Studies Group, (1981) *Women in Society: Interdisciplinary Essays*, London: Virago.

Caplan, A. (ed) (1978) *The Sociobiology Debate*, New York: Harper & Row.

Carneiro, R. (1981) 'Leslie White', in S. Silverman (ed.) *Totems and Teachers: Perspectives in the History of Anthropology*, New York: Columbia University Press.

Cassirer, E. (1951) *The Philosophy of Enlightenment*, Princeton, NJ: Princeton University Press.

Chomsky, N. (1959) 'Review of *Verbal Behaviour* by B.F. Skinner', *Language* 35.

—— (1972) *Language and Mind*, New York: Harcourt, Brace, Jovanovitch.

—— (1980) *Rules and Representations*, Oxford: Basil Blackwell.

Condillac, E. de (1974) *An Essay on the Origin of Human Knowledge*, New York: AMS Press.

Coward, R. (1983) *Patriarchal Precedents*, London: Routledge & Kegan Paul.

Cravens, H. (1978) *The Triumph of Evolution*, Pennsylvania: University of Pennsylvania Press.

Crocker, L. (1963) *Nature and Culture: Ethical Thought in the French Enlightenment*, Baltimore: The Johns Hopkins University Press.

Curtiss, S. (1977) *Genie: A Psycholinguistic Study of a Modern-Day 'Wild Child'*, New York: Academic Press.

Davis, K. (1948) *Human Society*, New York: Macmillan.

Derrida, J. (1970) 'Structure, sign, and play in the discourse of the human sciences', in R. Macksey, and E. Donato, (eds) *The Languages of Criticism and the Sciences of Man: the Structuralist Controversy*, Baltimore: The Johns Hopkins University Press.

Descartes, R. (1968) *Discourse on Method and the Meditations*, Harmondsworth: Penguin.

Desmond, A. (1979) *The Ape's Reflexion*, London: Quartet.

Dudley, E. and Novack, M. (eds) (1972) *The Wild Man Within*, Pittsburgh PA.: University of Pittsburgh Press.

Ferguson, J. (1975) *Utopias of the Classical World*, London: Thames & Hudson.

Findlay, J.N. (1974) *Plato: The Written and Unwritten Doctrines*, London: Routledge & Kegan Paul.

Ford, C.S. and Beach, F. (1952) *Patterns of Sexual Behaviour*, London: Methuen.

Formigari, L. (1974) 'Language and society in the late eighteenth century', *Journal of the History of Ideas* 35, 2.

Foucault, M. (1970) *The Order of Things*, London: Tavistock.

Fouts, R. and Rigby, R.L. (1980) 'Man-chimpanzee communication' in T.A. Sebeok and J.V. Sebeok. (eds) *Speaking of Apes: a Critical Anthology of Two-way Communication with Man*, New York: Plenum.

Freeman, D. (1983) *Margaret Mead and Samoa*, Cambridge Mass: Harvard University Press.

Freud, S. (1960) *Totem and Taboo*, London: Routledge & Kegan Paul.

—— (1977) *On Sexuality*, Harmondsworth: Penguin.

Gardner, H. (1974) *The Quest for Mind*, New York: Vintage.

Gardner, R.A. and Gardner, B.T. (1980) 'Comparative psychology and language acquisition' in T.A. Sebeok and J.V. Sebeok (eds) *Speaking of Apes: a Critical Anthology of Two-way Communication with Man*, New York: Plenum.

Gay, P. (1967) *The Enlightenment: an Interpretation*, Vol. 1 *The Rise of Modern Paganism*, London: Weidenfeld & Nicolson.

—— (1970) *The Enlightenment: an Intepretation*, Vol. 2, *The Science of Freedom*, London: Weidenfeld & Nicolson.

Glacken, C. (1976) *Traces on the Rhodian Shore*, Berkeley, California: University of California Press.

Glass, B. (ed) (1959) *Forerunners of Darwin*, Baltimore: The Johns Hopkins University Press.

Glucksman, M. (1974) *Structuralist Analysis in Contemporary Social Thought*, London: Routledge & Kegan Paul.

Goldenweiser, A. (1917) 'The Autonomy of the Social', *American Anthropologist* 19.

Goodall, J. (1974) *In the Shadow of Man*, London: Fontana.

Goody, J. (1977) *The Domestication of the Savage Mind*, Cambridge: Cambridge University Press.

Greene, J. (1959) *The Death of Adam: Evolution and its Impact on Western Thought*, Iowa: University of Iowa Press.

Griffin, G. (1981) *The Question of Animal Awareness: Evolutionary Continuity of Mental Experience*, New York: Rockefeller University Press.

Hacking, I. (1975) *Why Does Language Matter to Philosophy?*, Cambridge: Cambridge University Press.

Hampson, N. (1968) *The Enlightenment*, Harmondsworth: Penguin.

Harris, M. (1968) *The Rise of Anthropological Theory*, London: Routledge & Kegan Paul.

—— (1980) *Cultural Materialism*, New York: Vintage.

Hatch, E. (1973) *Theories of Man and Culture*, New York: Columbia University Press.

Hazard, P. (1953) *The European Mind*, London: Hollis and Carter.

Hine, E. McNiven (1979) *A Critical Study of Condillac's Traite des Systemes*, The Hague: Martinus Nijhoff.

Hirst, P. and Woolley, P. (1982) *Social Relations and Human Attributes*, London: Tavistock.

—— (1985) 'Nature and culture in social science: the demarcation of domains of being in eighteenth century and modern discourses', *Geoforum*, 16, 2.

Hobbes, T. (1981) *Leviathan*, Harmondsworth: Penguin.

Hodgen, M. (1964) *Early Anthropology in the Sixteenth and Seventeenth Centuries*, Pennsylvania: University of Pennsylvania Press.

Hofstadter, R. (1955) *Social Darwinism in American Thought*, Boston: Beacon Press.

Honour, H. (1975) *The New Golden Land: European Images of America from the Discoveries to the Present Time*, New York: Pantheon.

Husband, T. (1981) *The Wild Man: Mediaeval Myth and Symbolism*, New York: Metropolitan Museum of Art.

Hymes, D. (1976) 'Comments on Mounin' *Current Anthropology* 17, 1.

Janson, H. (1952) *Apes and Ape Lore in the Middle Ages*, London: Warburg Institute.

Jenkins, A. (1979) *The Social Theory of Claude Levi-Strauss*, London: Macmillan.

Jones, G. (1980) *Social Darwinism and English Thought*, Brighton: Harvester Press.

Kemp. J. (1937) *Diderot: Interpreter of Nature*, London: Lawrence & Wishart.

Konner, M. (1982) 'She and He', *Science* 82.

Kroeber, A.L. (1952) *The Nature of Culture*, Chicago: University of Chicago Press.

—— and Kluckhohn, C. (1952) 'Culture: a critical review of concepts and definitions', *Harvard, US Papers of the Peabody Museum of American Archaeology and Ethnology* 47.

Laidler, K. (1981) 'Take a look at yourself', *Guardian*, 12 November 1981.

Lane, H. (1979) *The Wild Boy of Aveyron*, London: Paladin.

—— and Pilling, R. (1978) *The Wild Boy of Burundi*, New York: Random House.

Langness, L.L. (1974) *The Study of Culture*, San Francisco: Chandler and Sharp.

Laplanche, J. and Pontalis, J-B (1973) *The Language of Psychoanalysis*, London: The Hogarth Press.

Leach, E. (1982) *Social Anthropology*, London: Fontana.

Lenneberg, E. (1967) *Biological Foundations of Language*, New York: Wiley.

Lesser, A. (1981) 'Franz Boas' in S. Silverman (ed.) *Totems and Teachers: Perspectives in the History of Anthropology*, New York: Columbia University Press.

Levi-Strauss, C. (1963) *Structural Anthropology*, vol. 1, London: Allen Lane.

—— (1964) *Totemism*, London: Merlin.

—— (1966) *The Savage Mind*, London: Weidenfeld & Nicolson.

—— (1969) *The Elementary Structures of Kinship*, London: Eyre and Spottiswoode.

Lieberman, P. (1976) 'Comments on Mounin', *Current Anthropology* 17, 1.

Limber, J. (1980) 'Language in Child and Chimp' in T.A. Sebeok and J.V. Sebeok (eds) *Speaking of Apes: a Critical Anthology of Two-way Communication with Man*, New York: Plenum.

Linden, E. (1976) *Apes, Men and Language*, New York: Pelican.

Locke, J. (1966) *The Second Treatise of Government*, edited with an introduction by J.W. Gough, Oxford: Basil Blackwell.

Lopez, B. (1978) *Of Wolves and Men*, New York: Charles.

Lovejoy, A.O. (1948) *Essays in the History of Ideas*, Baltimore: The Johns Hopkins University Press.

—— (1964) *The Great Chain of Being*, Cambridge, Mass: Harvard University Press.

—— (1965) *Essays in the History of Ideas*, Cambridge, Mass. Harvard University Press.

MacCormack, C. (1980) 'Nature, culture, and gender: a critique', in MacCormack and M. Strathern. *Nature, Culture and Gender*, Cambridge: Cambridge University Press.

—— and Strathern, M. (1980) *Nature, Culture and Gender*, Cambridge: Cambridge University Press.

Macksey, R and Donato, E (eds) (1970) *The Languages of Criticism and the Sciences of Man: the Structuralist Controversy*. Baltimore: The Johns Hopkins University Press.

Malinowski, B. (1944) *A Scientific Theory of Culture*, Chappel Hill: University of North Carolina Press.

Malson, L. (1972) *Wolf Children*, London: New Left Books.

Manila, G.J. (1982) *Marcos: Wild Child of the Sierra Morena*, London: Souvenir Press.

Mason, J.H. (1979) *The Indispensable Rousseau*, London: Quartet.

Mazur, O. (1980) *The Wild Man in the Spanish Renaissance and Golden Age Theatre*, Ann Arbor Michigan: University Microfilms International.

McClean, C. (1979) *The Wolf Children*, Harmondsworth: Penguin Books.

Mead, G.H. (1934) *Mind, Self and Society*, Chicago: University of Chicago Press.

Midgley, M. (1980a) *Beast and Man*, London: Methuen.

—— (1980b) 'Rival Fatalism' in A. Montagu (ed.). *Sociobiology Examined*, Oxford: Oxford University Press.

Montagu, A. (ed) (1980) *Sociobiology Examined*, Oxford: Oxford University Press.

Moravia, S. (1980) 'The Enlightenment and the sciences of man', *History of Science Journal* XVIII.

Mounin, G. (1976) 'Language, Communication, Chimpanzees' *Current Anthropology* 17, 1.

Nadler, R.D. and Braggio, J.T. (1974) 'Sex and species differences in captive-reared juvenile chimpanzees and orang-utans', *Journal of Human Revolution* 3.

Novack, M. (1972) 'The wild man comes to tea' in E. Dudley and M. Novack (eds) *The Wild Man Within*, Pittsburgh, Pa.: University of Pittsburgh Press.

Ogburn, W. (1959) 'The wild boy of Agra', *American Journal of Sociology* LXIV, 5.

Pagden, A. (1982) *The Fall of Natural Man: The American Indian and the Origins of Comparative Ethnology*, Cambridge: Cambridge University Press.

Patterson, F.G. (1978) 'The gestures of a gorilla: language acquisition in another pongid', *Brain and Language* 5.

Plato (1970) *The Dialogues of Plato*. Vol 3 *Timaeus and Other Dialogues*, Trans. by Benjamin Jowett, London: Sphere.

Reynolds, P. (1981) *The Evolution of Human Behaviour*, Berkeley, California: University of California Press.

Reynolds, V. (1980) *The Biology of Human Action*, San Francisco: Freeman.

Rossi, I. (ed) (1974) *The Unconscious in Culture*, New York: Dutton.

Rousseau, J-J (1973) *The Social Contract and Discourses*, Trans. with an introduction by G.D.H. Cole, London: J.M. Dent & Sons.

Sahlins, M. (1976) *Culture and Practical Reason*, Chicago: University of Chicago Press.

—— (1977) *The Use and Abuse of Biology*, London: Tavistock.

Sandars, N-K (ed) (1972) *The Epic of Gilgamesh*, Harmondsworth: Penguin.

Sapir, E. (1917) 'Do We Need a "Super-Organic'?', *American Anthropologist* 19.

Savage-Rumbaugh, E.S., Rumbaugh, D.M. and Boyson, S. (1980) 'Linguistically mediated tool-use and exchange by chimpanzees' in T.A. Sebeok and J.V. Sebeok (eds) *Speaking of Apes: a Critical Anthology of Two-way Communication with Man*, New York: Plenum.

Sebeok, T.A. and Sebeok, J.U. (eds) (1980) *Speaking of Apes: a Critical Anthology of Two-Way Communication with Man*, New York: Plenum.

Shackley, M.L. (1983) *Wildmen: Yeti, Sasquatch and the Neanderthal Enigma*, London: Thames & Hudson.

Shattuck, R. (1980) *The Forbidden Experiment*, New York: Farrar Strauss Giroux.

Shorey, P. (1933) *What Plato Said*, Chicago: University of Chicago Press.

Silverman, S. (ed) (1981) *Totems and Teachers: Perspectives in the History of Anthropology*, New York: Columbia University Press.

Singer, M. (1968) Entry on 'Culture' in *International Encyclopaedia of the Social Sciences*, New York: Macmillan.

Smith, B. (1960) *European Vision and the South Pacific*, Oxford: Oxford University Press.

Smith, J.M. (1975) *The Theory of Evolution*, Harmondsworth: Penguin.

Stam. J. (1976) *Inquiries into the Origin of Language*, New York: Harper & Row.

Stocking, G. (1982) *Race, Culture and Evolution: Essays in the History of Anthropology*, Chicago: University of Chicago Press.

Strathern, M. (1980) 'No nature, no culture: the Hagen Case', in MacCormack and M. Strathern. *Nature, Culture and Gender*, Cambridge: Cambridge Press.

Street, B. (1975) *The Savage in Literature: Representations of 'Primitive' Society in English Fiction 1858-1920*, London: Routledge & Kegan Paul.

Suomi, S.J. Harlow, H.F. and Novack, M.H. (1974) 'Reversal of social deficits produced by isolation rearing in monkeys', *Journal of Human Evolution* 3.

Symcox, G. (1972) 'The wild man's return' in E. Dudley and M. Novack (eds) *The Wild Man Within*, Pittsburgh, Pa.: University of Pittsburgh Press.

Symons, D. (1979) *The Evolution of Human Sexuality*, Oxford: Oxford University Press.

Tacitus (1970) *Germania*, Harmondsworth: Penguin.

Terrace, H. (1980) *Nim*, London: Eyre Methuen.

Tylor, E.B. (1913) *Primitive Culture*, Vol. 1, London.

Walker, S. (1982) *Animal Thought*, London: Routledge & Kegan Paul.

Weisstein, N. (1982) 'Tired of arguing about biological inferiority', Ms. November 1982.

White, H. (1972) 'The Forms of Wildness' in E. Dudley and M. Novack (eds). *The Wild Man Within*, Pittsburgh, Pa.: University of Pittsburgh Press.

White, L. (1949) *The Science of Culture*, New York: Grove Press.

Whitney, L. (1934) *Primitivism and the Idea of Progress*, Baltimore: The Johns Hopkins University Press.

Willey, B. (1980) *The Eighteenth Century Background: Studies on the Idea of Nature in the Thought of the Period* London: Chatto & Windus.

Wittkower, R. (1975) 'Marvels of the East: a study in the history of monsters', in R. Wittkower, *Allegory and Migration of Symbols*, London: Thames & Hudson.

Wokler, R. (1976) 'Tyson and Buffon on the orang-utan' *Studies on Voltaire and the Eighteenth Century*, 155: 2301-19.

—— (1978) 'Perfectible apes in decadent cultures: Rousseau's anthropology revisited', *Daedalus*, 107, 3: 107-34.

Wolf, E. (1981) 'A.L. Kroeber' in S. Silverman (ed.) *Totems and Teachers: Perspectives in the History of Anthropology*, New York: Columbia University Press.

Zingg, R. (1940) 'Feral man and extreme cases of isolation', *American Journal of Psychology*, 43.

Index